Brain-Based Worship

BRAIN-BASED WORSHIP

Remembering the Mind-Body Connection

Paula Champion-Jones

WESTBOW
PRESS
A DIVISION OF THOMAS NELSON
& ZONDERVAN

Copyright © 2014 Paula Champion-Jones.

All rights reserved. No part of this book may be used or reproduced by any means, graphic, electronic, or mechanical, including photocopying, recording, taping or by any information storage retrieval system without the written permission of the publisher except in the case of brief quotations embodied in critical articles and reviews.

All Scripture quotations, unless otherwise indicated, are taken from the Holy Bible, New International Reader's Version®, NIrV® Copyright © 1995, 1996, 1998 by Biblica, Inc.™ Used by permission of Zondervan. All rights reserved worldwide. www.zondervan.com The "NIrV" and "New International Reader's Version" are trademarks registered in the United States Patent and Trademark Office by Biblica, Inc.™

WestBow Press books may be ordered through booksellers or by contacting:

WestBow Press
A Division of Thomas Nelson & Zondervan
1663 Liberty Drive
Bloomington, IN 47403
www.westbowpress.com
1 (866) 928-1240

Because of the dynamic nature of the Internet, any web addresses or links contained in this book may have changed since publication and may no longer be valid. The views expressed in this work are solely those of the author and do not necessarily reflect the views of the publisher, and the publisher hereby disclaims any responsibility for them.

Any people depicted in stock imagery provided by Thinkstock are models, and such images are being used for illustrative purposes only.
Certain stock imagery © Thinkstock.

ISBN: 978-1-4908-5170-9 (sc)
ISBN: 978-1-4908-5169-3 (hc)
ISBN: 978-1-4908-5171-6 (e)

Library of Congress Control Number: 2014916423

Printed in the United States of America.

WestBow Press rev. date: 10/03/2014

For Joe,
Who made it possible

"What's in it for me?" "How will I look if I do this?" This is our preferred way of seeing reality. It has become the "hardware" of almost all Western people, even those who think of themselves as Christians, because the language of institutional religion is largely dualistic itself. It is a way of teaching that has totally taken over in the last five hundred years. It has confused information with enlightenment, mind with soul, and thinking with experiencing. But they are two very different paths.

- Richard Rohr

Contents

Foreword ix
Introduction: How Bad Can It Possibly Be? xiii

Chapter 1:   Disremembering 1
Chapter 2:   Forgetting To Remember 16
Chapter 3:   Dismembered 28
Chapter 4:   Designed To Re-Member 37
Chapter 5:   Menaces To Memory 46
Chapter 6:   Remember To Release Control 60
Chapter 7:   Multisensory Memories 69
Chapter 8:   Memory Making And Emotions 82
Chapter 9:   Storied Memory 91
Chapter 10: Metaphorical Memory 109
Chapter 11: Remembering As A Team 121

Memorandum: A Conclusion 135
Bibliography 161
About the Author 167

Foreword

To my everlasting shame, I did not appreciate my professor. James B. Ashbrook and I got off on the wrong foot when part of my first-year "orientation" at The Rochester Center for Theological Studies (Colgate Rochester/Bexley Hall/Crozer/St. Bernard's) was a "no-exit relationship" that pitted a mountain-culture white southerner (me) with an urban-culture African American (Edward Wheeler). The experiment was research for a project Ashbrook was conducting. He subsequently wrote up our "story" in a book (without our knowledge, although he did change the dates and names). As a psychologist of religion, Professor Ashbrook hailed from what I deemed at the time as that soft, amorphous "D" division of the curriculum, while I was a stalwart Ph.D. student in the hard-science "B" division discipline of history. As a psychologist, Ashbrook was always asking "how do you feel about this?" while I was more interested in asking "how do you think about that?" As a presumed scholar of the intellect rather than the affect—a difference which back then made history appear downright algorithmic by comparison—I only took the courses from him that were required, and kept my distance even when he made overtures of collegiality in my direction.

One of the worst things you can say of anyone is that "Greatness Passed By," and they missed it. Every passing year, I realize more and more just how much I "missed." Long before Jill Bolte-Taylor and Iain McGilchrist there was James B. Ashbrook. Ashbrook was the first scholar to bring together brain science and theology, the first theologian to explore the ramifications of the left and the right hemispheres of the brain not merely having different functions but also different insights, values and priorities, and the first psychologist to pioneer a burgeoning field of study called neurotheology.

Neurotheology is generating some of the most important questions being asked in my lifetime. As neurotheology converses and cross-pollinates with neuroscience, psychology and cognitive science, it is causing fundamental shifts in our understanding of how people learn and live. Ashbrook's explorations of the different processing of the left and right brain took some preliminary steps to address the biggest challenge in cognitive studies: how is it that physical processes in the brain give rise to subjective experience. And vice versa, what if theology should be the Holy Spirit working its way through your brain?

"Navigational Nineties" is one of the best suggestions for naming the unnamed 90s decade when we started learning how to navigate our genes, navigate our brains, navigate silicon. This book is about navigating our souls and communities. Dr. Champion-Jones champions a brain-based learning paradigm that inspires memorable teaching, as well as incubates learners who are both highly motivated to learn and who are more likely to change long-held attitudes and actions. As you follow her research, you will shake your head in wonderment at the power of brain-based applications to lead to life transformation.

What is more, brain-based strategies have huge implications for those entrusted with the church's teaching ministry. When utilized reverently and appropriately in worship, they generate a learning environment where God can be encountered in ways that go beyond intellectual knowing. Brain-based methods encourage a more tangible, embodied faith that is expressed in narratives and metaphors (narraphors), signs and symbols. Worship becomes less about what God is saying through the preacher and more about what God is saying to each person, less about conformity and more about encounter, less about church as institution and more about church as living organism.

If you are looking for the latest church growth method or for an easy formula for worship, this book isn't it. If you are willing to unlearn old habits and skills that worked in the industrial age, express Truth in non-traditional ways, invest in creative people, and even abandon part of your seminary education to worship in a new playground, the playground of the Spirit, you may discover that you can usher your people deeper into conversations with God.

If the church ignores how the brain works, she does so at her own risk. *Brain-Based Worship* delivers a usable, effective strategy for those involved in worship planning and execution. Written in reader-friendly language, it offers an easy-to-understand explanation of the relation between teaching methods, transformational learning, and the way God originally designed the brain to function.

The first description of worship in the Bible resulted in murder. Cain—the first human conceived—was a murderer. He grew jealous of the praise offering his brother Abel was giving to God, and killed him. The "worship wars" are properly named. In its worship, the church wears its soul on its sleeve. This book is sleeve surgery for a church that needs the peace that only the mind of Christ can give.

Leonard Sweet
E. Stanley Jones Professor, Drew Theological School
Distinguished Visiting Professor, George Fox Evangelical Seminary

Introduction:
How Bad Can It Possibly Be?

Don't let them fool you. Polls may report that 85 percent of Americans claim to be Catholic, Protestant, or Jewish, but when answering questions on a poll, we all tend to say what makes us look good. It's called creating a 'holy halo.' People do the same thing in other ways—subtracting fifteen pounds from their weight when renewing a driver's license or using a five-year old photo as a profile pic on a social media site. Deviating slightly from the truth can seem harmless when it comes to creating a good first impression.

That is why the articulation of religious identity has little to do with actual behavior. In reality, less than twenty percent of Americans regularly attend church.[1] Most of us could compare the weekly attendance in our own church to our membership roll and quickly confirm that many who claim they are affiliated with us are making empty claims.

In June of 2013, The Huffington Post announced that increasing numbers of Americans are claiming no religious affiliation whatsoever when asked to state their religious identity. Uninterested in the institutionalized church, unimpressed by credentialed clergy, and with no strong attachment to the Bible, they have adopted new standards for what is sacred. "The religious worlds in the contemporary and future United States are robust and capacious, providing an abundance

---

[1] Rebecca Barnes and Lindy Lowery, "Seven Startling Facts: An Up Close Look at Church Attendance in America," *Church Leaders*, February 2013. http://www.churchleaders.com/pastors/pastor-articles/139575-7-startling-facts-an-up-close-look-at-church-attendance-in-america.html (accessed July 7, 2013).

of spiritual possibilities found in unexpected places like drum circles and meditation exercises, sports events and other expressions from popular culture. It is a brave new world for religious Americans who are increasingly unhinged from traditional authorities and institutions."[2]

Dynamic intimate knowledge of God is being replaced with spiritual trivialities, denominational legalities, and strong political opinions based on the propaganda of civil religion. Vibrant personal familiarity with the Creator can only germinate from seeds of regular, unpretentious, blatantly honest conversations with God that have been deeply rooted and grounded in the soil of Scripture. Both seed and soil are becoming more rare.

We have all heard the predictions of the doom and decline of the Church in the 21st century. Many of us are personally witnessing that decline right now, even as we pour our own blood, sweat, and tears into studying Scripture, shaping select passages into organized, coherent sermons, preparing worship services, and tirelessly serving our communities. We take our calling seriously, yet there are days when all our effort seems pointless. Even as we determinedly labor to grow the Kingdom of God, we continue to lose ground. Apathy among church members grows while attendance falls. The majority of our young adults, craving awkward authenticity more than plastic perfection, are deserting the mainline church as soon as they leave the nest.

Experience eventually teaches even the most optimistic of us those congregants who are living lives that daily manifest Christ are in the minority. In a typical week, we find ourselves refereeing petty skirmishes between committee members or serving as a conflict manager for a divided staff fighting territorial battles. Committed church members go to war with each other over trivialities. Key lay leaders are caught up in scandals. Spousal abuse, substance abuse, divorce, and promiscuous sex are just as real within the Church as anywhere else. Called to be ministers of reconciliation, we are regularly required to witness disintegrating relationships in families and faith families.

---

[2] Gary Laderman, "The Rise of Religious 'Nones' Indicates the End of Religion as We Know It," *The Huffington Post,* March 20, 2013. http://www.huffingtonpost.com/gary-laderman/the-rise-of-religious-non_b_2913000.html (accessed February 2, 2014).

In spite of the fact that Jesus made it clear that our relationship with God is inseparable from our relationship with others, we just don't seem to be able to relate without competition and ego getting in the way. Relinquishing hard-earned personal privilege is seldom high on anyone's agenda. "Taking the form of a servant" may sound good on paper, but in our day-to-day life, it's just not as appealing as flexing one's muscles in the midst of a power struggle.[3]

Church statistics are grim, but they only tell part of the story. The emotional and spiritual health of the clergy is under assault. Because we don't understand why our effort often returns to us with no return, we blame ourselves for the downward spiraling trend as we secretly label ourselves as failures. Some studies show that up to seventy percent of clergy drop out of ministry within the first five years of entering.[4] Other findings reveal that seventy percent admit to fighting depression. Forty-eight percent think their work is hazardous to their family's well being. Some 1,500 pastors leave the ministry each month due to moral failure, spiritual burnout, or contention in their churches.[5] Clergy have never been more discouraged. We may not admit it out loud, but we know it in our gut. The old ways of doing church are no longer working.

Unfortunately, some of the new ways seem gimmicky and tasteless. Does God really need the smoke and mirrors of a rock concert just to get noticed? In our heart of hearts, we know God deserves better than to be peddled like an infomercial product. C.S. Lewis wrote of the inappropriateness of using gimmicks in worship. "A good shoe is a shoe you don't notice. Good reading becomes possible when you need not consciously think about eyes, or light, or print, or spelling. The perfect church service would be one we were almost unaware of; our attention would have been on God. But every novelty prevents this. It fixes our

---

[3] Philippians 2:7

[4] Carol Howard Merrit, "Tribal Church: Perspectives on the Young Clergy Crisis," *The Christian Century*, December 10, 2011. http://www.christiancentury.org/blogs/archive2011-2012/perspectives-yong-clergy-crisis (accessed July 5, 2013).

[5] Eugene Cho, "Death by Ministry," Eugene Cho Blog, August 11, 2010, http://eugenecho.com/2010/08/11/death-by-ministry (accessed July 14, 2013).

attention on the service itself; and thinking about worship is a different thing from worshipping."

So what are our choices? We have several. We can continue to do things just as we have always done and pray for a miracle. We can pull out all the stops—employing bells and whistles and shiny, happy people—using any ploy necessary to grab attention. We can call it quits, believing the inevitable is upon us, or we can aggressively search for better teaching methods, ones that are both scripturally endorsed and will speak to our time and our situation. The exciting news is that because of recent findings in the disciplines of neuroscience and cognitive science, we know these tools exist, have always existed, and are free for the taking! If we choose to pick them up and put them to use, I am convinced that the Holy Spirit will ensure that the Christian church is not just another antiquated relic that existed a long time ago in a galaxy far, far away.

Chapter 1

DISREMEMBERING

The sofa upon which I sat was one of several cast-off specimens donated to the church when the original owner decided it was time for an upgrade. Predictably, it ended up in the one room where there could never be too many tacky sofas––the student minister's office. I was there to say a reluctant goodbye to our student minister, Brady. He had recently turned in his resignation, having taken a similar position at another church. As he packed up his office, we laughed and reminisced about the time that we had served together.

As we talked, our extroverted senior pastor, Mitch, strode into the room, plopped down on a sofa, and joined the chat. No problem there–– Brady's office would be a veritable turnstile of well-wishing friends all day. He was thoroughly enjoying the attention.

After a few minutes, however, Mitch hijacked the conversation, taking us on an uncomfortable detour. Speaking to Brady in the same tone a father might use to correct a wayward child, he lectured, "You know you've just moved up to the big league, don't you? That's a *First* church you're going to. They won't let you get away with some of the junk you pull here. They're gonna expect a professional. You're gonna have to completely change the way you dress. You can't go to work there wearing ratty jeans and a faded T-shirt. Sandals won't cut it either. Before next week, you need to go buy a few button-down shirts, some nice casual pants, and a pair of real shoes if you think you're going to survive there."

I listened to his well-meaning advice as long as I could before interjecting my thoughts—after all, I would be disagreeing with my boss. Finally, unable to bite my tongue any longer, I interrupted, "Mitch, what you're saying is driving me crazy. First of all, Brady will be working with youth; jeans and T-shirts are practically required. But more importantly, what about that guy who told us that we shouldn't waste our time worrying about what we're going to eat or what we're going to wear?"

Mitch didn't even blink before asking, "What guy?"

In that moment, Mitch had disremembered Jesus. The word *disremember* may sound to the modern ear like an inaccurate use of language, but it has been used since the seventeenth century. To disremember is to fail to remember. Mitch failed to remember that Jesus advised us not to waste time worrying about what we are going to eat or how we are going to dress. It would be easier to fault my boss if I didn't disremember Jesus on regular occasions, failing to respond with love to a critic or to appreciate the kind of treasure that really counts in this life.

Disremembering Worship

The church is presently facing a disremembering crisis. Just because a church can give a theologically correct definition of worship does not mean it is worshipping. Nor does the fact that the church advertises weekly worship services mean that it's worshipping. Even if it employs a full-time minister of worship, there is no guarantee that worship in spirit and in truth is occurring. That's because we are living in an age that has disremembered what worship actually is, confusing worshipping God with conducting or attending a worship service.

Now, worship services aren't bad things at all. They can be the perfect balm to soothe a painfully throbbing conscience, washing away guilt like a whirlpool bath washes away stress. A weekly outing to your church's hallowed halls can give you the inspiration you need to get through yet another trying week. Many attest to the fact that regularly attending church makes the difficulties of life easier to bear. Joining in rousing renditions of a few of your favorite songs can lift your spirits quicker than almost anything. Spending a couple of hours with kindred spirits who share your values is always good for the soul. In addition, frequent churchgoers have larger social support networks, and good social support is directly tied to better health. Yes, attending church comes with a surplus of benefits.

Worship, on the other hand, is a horse of a totally different color. Worship is not about making life easier, refueling for another week, disposing of annoying guilt, or connecting with friends. It's about connecting with God––and few things can make a person feel less comfortable than an encounter with pure, unadulterated divinity.

Worship can be affirming and uplifting, but just as often, it's unsettling. It reminds us of who we are, who God is, and how we should consequently relate to a God who is far superior to anything we can imagine. Worship reminds us that God goes to extremes to bridge the gulf that separates us from Him and from each other. Like Isaiah, a person who encounters God in unpretentious worship is left spiritually, intellectually, emotionally, and even physically overwhelmed. Isaiah's response should be our response: *"Woe to me!" I cried. "I am ruined! For I am a man of unclean lips, and I live among a people of unclean lips, and my eyes have seen the King, the Lord Almighty."* (Isaiah 6:5)

Even as we read Isaiah's response, I'm convinced that our minds unknowingly tone his words down a few notches in an attempt to prevent spiritual trauma. Try to imagine this––when Isaiah encountered God, Isaiah was left staggering in dismay, tearing at his robes in regret and shame, shrieking in shock-tinted grief, "No! No! No! I've looked God in the face! I know I'm doomed! I've condemned myself with my own words. Compared to God's beauty, truth, and goodness, I'm worthless! Totally worthless! And all the people around me––they're no different! We're all doomed!"

Isaiah's cry was one of utter despair. He made no excuses. He never attempted to justify his many failed attempts at righteousness. He didn't compare himself to others. He just recognized that he was in the same sinking boat as everyone else. If one went down, they were all going down. Instead of pleading his case, Isaiah changed his life, offering it to God in a lifetime of worship that would be expressed in service to others.

That's what worship does. It begins when we encounter the living God who is revealed in his written word (Scripture) and his living Word (Jesus Christ). In his presence, we come face-to-face with our own brokenness. Only then can God move us to grieve for the brokenness of those around us. That kind of holy heartache impels us to action as we begin to glimpse God-possibilities in our lives and in the lives of others. Ironically, that same heartache can also lead to joyful expressions of who we are in Christ, expressions that manifest themselves as dancing, singing, holy play, sharing our resources, and even speaking in tongues.

To *worship* means to "Love the Lord your God with all your heart and with all your soul and with all your mind and with all strength." (Luke 10:27) To love God with your heart, soul, mind and strength takes on a little different meaning when we go back to the way the words were used in the first century. Words have a way of changing over time. Think about the word *rock*. Sixty years ago no one would have equated the word with a genre of music. Words used by biblical writers have had thousands of years to shift in meaning.

In the language of Scripture, the word *heart* has a lot more to do with the human will than with emotions. Therefore, to love God with our heart is to love him with our actions and choices. We make choices daily that indicate what we esteem most—God's desires for us or our own ideas about what we need. In making God-honoring choices, we are loving God with our hearts.

To love God with our soul is to love him with our emotions. Again, the meaning has shifted. Twenty-first-century Americans tend to think of the soul as the incorporeal and eternal part of the individual. In earlier times, soul had to do with the emotional capacity of humans. You can see this reflected in David's question, "Why, my soul, are you downcast?" (Psalm 42:5) He is writing of an emotional low in life. When we love God with our soul, we are emotionally involved with him on every level.

To love God with our mind is a little less confusing. It means to engage our intellect as we worship. When we spend time with God in prayer and Scripture study, we are loving him with our mind, growing a relationship with the one who took the initiative to begin that relationship with us. We can only get to know a person if he or she chooses to reveal who they are to us, if he or she spends time with us and makes himself or herself vulnerable to us. We cannot force a healthy relationship. We have to be invited into one. That is exactly what God does with the written Truth of Scripture and the living Truth of Jesus Christ. He discloses himself to humanity, and in doing so, invites humanity into relationship.

Finally, to love God with our strength has to do with getting our whole body involved in the act of loving him, of allowing the physical aspect of who we are to join in the fun. Worship in biblical times was full-bodied worship. Multiple words describe such worshipful acts as singing, dancing, rejoicing. the raising of hands, shouting, clapping, kneeling, greeting each other with a holy kiss (though in our culture, hugs are more acceptable), prostrating oneself in prayer, bowing down, lifting the face, verbally questioning God, physically experiencing fear or awe—the list is almost endless. Unlike the pew-potatoes of our day, worshippers were actively moving and interacting with him.

Thus, Luke 10:27 tells us that fully loving God means involving him in the *choices* we make, in our *thought patterns*, and with unapologetic, uninhibited *emotional* and *bodily* involvement. When all four aspects of our identities regularly engage with God in worship, we encounter him in life-changing ways. Even though encounters with the divine can happen anywhere, anyplace, and at anytime, life-changing meetings with God are all too rare these days. They should be common occurrences in our weekly worship services.

Counting the Cost

Worship design is a highly underrated but tremendously rewarding art form. Done well, its execution honors God by aiding others to experience his presence and power. The book you now hold is written in the hopes that you can learn to design just such worship experiences.

No, you cannot compel anyone to worship; the Holy Spirit blows where the Holy Spirit blows. What you can do is cut down all the fences, hedgerows, and trees that might hinder the force of the wind when it does begin to gust. You can construct wind tunnels that will channel the breeze to hot, dry corners of your community. You can create an environment that rejoices in breezy days, ones that allows the air current to scatter grace as naturally as a summer breeze spreads the fuzzy seeds of a dandelion. If you are on a church staff in any position, or if you are a layperson who serves in any capacity planning or executing worship, your most important job—far more important than planning mission projects, producing musicals, publicizing retreats, or projecting budgets—is to enable your congregation to feel the advancing wind of God. When the stage is set with care, skill, and a little creativity, they will discover the Spirit playing in their hair and lifting their hearts to gaze upon God as surely as a spring breeze lifts a kite heavenward.

If you are looking for easy answers to the question, "How do I grow a church?" you probably shouldn't bother reading any further—but then again, you probably aren't the kind of person who takes the easy path in life. If you did, you would never have gone into ministry. Likely, you've already figured out that God seldom traffics in easy answers.

I assume that you are serving in your particular role at your church because, like Isaiah, you have tasted God's unmatched holiness, exquisite grace, and inexhaustible mercy. You have come face to face with your own brokenness and have experienced the healing love of Jesus. You genuinely want others to experience the same boundless wonder you have known.

Like so many others in ministry, your soul may ache for those in your charge, wanting them to lay hold of the abundant life—the life they may confidently talk about in class, may even dream about in private, but never actually anticipate enjoying in reality. Possibly you envision individuals in your church being noticeably transformed into the image of Jesus Christ. Perhaps you ache for people who hunger for holiness. Quite conceivably, you dream of men, women, and children whose lives exhibit that their spirits have been awakened and energized by a living God.

It's not impossible for those dreams to become realities. Throughout history, there have been sporadic periods when spiritual awakenings have occurred, times when the Church was restored to a life-giving and impassioned relationship with God after a long period of decline and corruption. These periods of spiritual awakening have always begun after several previous generations lost sight of what it meant to follow Jesus.

During the dark times preceding the renewals, the institutional church had allowed herself to be seduced by culture, and in so doing, she exchanged what could have been a deep, empowering relationship with God for personal power and for conscience-soothing religious rituals that pacified the ego but slow-rotted the soul. Much like the Pharisee who thanked God that he was not like other men, the self-satisfied, self-important church was being slowly asphyxiated by the fumes of her own pride.

Whenever this happens, God responds by raising up a new generation to restore true worship, a generation that rejects power and empty ritual at high personal cost. I believe we are on the cusp of just such a time right now. I say this because every day I talk to young people who have been disillusioned by the institutionalized church but who have not given up on God, college students who are more interested in being real than in going through the prescribed motions, youthful parents who want their children to know God but who are afraid to entrust them to an organization that makes the news weekly with scandal and immorality. I see the hunger in their eyes for Truth with a capital 'T,' for meaning that goes beyond acquisition of material possessions, and for a foundation that is unshakable in shaky times. I believe God intends to use today's generation to reboot the Church and to carry his Kingdom forward. Why now and not 20 years ago? I have absolutely no idea. I only know that God will start somewhere and signs are all pointing in the direction of impending renewal.

That said, for those of us who want to be part of a fresh movement of the Holy Spirit, there will be a cost. There is always a cost if you are to be used by and for God. The bad news is that the more entrenched you are in the institutional church and its hierarchical power structure, the higher the price will seem. The good news is that for those who long to see the reign of God extended, no price can possibly be too high.

The fact is that renewal of the Church can only happen through reform. *Reform* may be a less intimidating way of saying *sweeping change*, but it is change nevertheless. For those who are satisfied with the status quo, and many are, *change* is a synonym for *heresy*. Those who resist change will have a difficult time adjusting to the coming revival.

If you are already aware that you have a difficult time dealing with change, you will need to make some conscious choices beginning straightaway. Will you put this book down now because it makes you feel uncomfortable? Or will you begin to pray for a heart so inflamed with the love of God that the thought of change threatens you less than the thought of displeasing God? That is a decision only you can make, and Christ did counsel us to count the cost before embarking on action. Depending on what you value, the cost could be considerable.

Cost #1: Accept Who You Are

Even though it may go against the grain, whether you are a pastor, a minister of music, a student minster, or a minister of education, if you want to play a role in church renewal, one of the costs may well be the acceptance of a new identity, a more realistic identity. Ask yourself who you are. If your immediate answer consists of your job title, you may have already forgotten who you are.

Your job title may give you a certain amount of prestige in your community. Some assume that they must treat you with respect. Others shower love on you, God's representative, as a way of showing love to God. You may even stand in awe of yourself, super-hero that you are, spending your life fighting against dark powers. Or you may be cut from more humble cloth, wondering how God could have possibly chosen to use you. In any case, you need to remember that your job title is not who you are.

Regardless of what title goes into the Church bulletin beside your name, you are first and foremost a follower of Jesus. Being his devoted disciple means you can never anchor your identity to anything but Him—and He will be constantly and consistently changing you into his image. If you still believe exactly what you believed five years ago, you are probably not following very closely.

Second, as a follower of Jesus you are also a teacher. You may be teaching in a formal setting, in the home, on the job, or during involvement in community activities, but no matter where you are, no matter what you are doing, the way you live your life teaches what you value. People can (or cannot) see the love of God shining through you. Their impression of God is based on their impression of you.

At the first seminary I attended, it was considered a slap in the face for pastors to be complimented for their teaching ability. A hard and fast, almost uncrossable line was drawn between the gifts of teaching and preaching. Because they were considered different disciplines, those who pursued them walked different degree paths. Pastors departed seminary with a Master of Divinity degree. Most ministers of education, student pastors, and children's ministers walked out the door with a Master of Religious Education. Pastors preached; everyone else 'only' taught.

Local church tradition further demarcated clergy and laity. Lay people were encouraged to *teach* other lay people in classrooms and in homes. Occasionally, one would be invited to give their testimony during a worship service––but what they did was never referred to as *preaching*. Professionally trained pastors, on the other hand, *preached*. They preached from behind pulpits during worship services, exegeting Scripture prophetically (at least we all liked to think we exegeted Scripture prophetically). Of course, we never verbalized the self-important belief, but we had been trained to assume that the role of *preacher* was a superior role to that of mere *teacher*.

In today's world, when we think of a teacher, we inevitably imagine textbooks, yellow number-2 pencils, desks, standardized tests, and grades. The concept of *teacher* is so thoroughly professionalized that when someone uses the word, it's automatically assumed that they are talking about an individual who possesses an advanced degree in some branch of education, who has been certified by the state, and who teaches in an elementary school, middle school, high school, or university. That, however, is a very limited view of what it means to be a teacher. Some of the most influential teachers in history have never taught in a traditional setting.

If, when choosing terms to describe Jesus, your mind first goes to words like *Lord, Savior, King, Son of God,* or *Redeemer,* you may need to reconsider. During Jesus' life, when others addressed him, they used the word *teacher* more often than any other word.[1] Others address Jesus some ninety times in the Gospels. Sixty of those times, he is called *teacher*. His disciples consistently referred to him as *teacher*. Matthew writes that because he *taught* as one having authority, he astounded his listeners. His last command to his followers was to *teach* the Gospel as they went into the world.

If the designation of *teacher* was good enough for Jesus, it should be good enough for those of us who have been entrusted with his teaching ministry. In spite of popular perception, and in spite of the denial of many who hold the title, pastors are, and always have been, teachers—teachers whose subject matter focuses on the art of living the Christ-centered life. Because we are responsible for teaching the most important subject matter of all time, we should be eager to develop our own teaching skills. We can only do this if we are willing to reconsider much of what we think we already know about teaching.

In a not-so-distant time, teaching was considered to be an exercise in drilling concepts into the brain of a fellow human. Although that type of teaching may have resulted in the correct answers on tests, it did not lead to transformation. If simply knowing the right intellectual information changed people, I would be twenty-five pounds lighter. Teaching that relied on the lecture method led to parroting words like—well—like a parrot.

Jesus was never overly impressed by those who could parrot all the right answers or who could execute a good impersonation of holiness, nor did he speak reassuringly about those who claimed him as Lord but who did not follow in his footsteps. He persistently taught with the goal of inner transformation. At no point do we see him encouraging surface change. If he had been satisfied with that, he would have never allowed the rich young ruler to walk away.

Following his example, those who plan worship should be less interested in using the worship hour to convey intellectual information about God, morals, ethics, or behavior, and more interested in using that time to enable those participating to meet with a God who is in the business of transforming humans.

---

[1] For a few examples, see Matthew 5:2, 7:29, Mark 1:21–22, 4:2, Luke 4:15, 20:1, John 7:14, 8:2.

Cost #2: Unlearn Invalid Information

Paying the price for a spiritually renewed congregation may also mean that you have to turn your back on some key parts of your very expensive seminary education. Earlier I noted the superior attitude we pastors can occasionally assume because of our called-by-God profession and our extensive seminary education. Even when we know the truth about ourselves in the recesses of our hearts, we all inadvertently find ourselves thinking we are 'special' at times. If at any point we start to feel like the resident religious expert, we need to take a step back and remind ourselves that when Jesus called his followers, he did not call any religious professional to be his disciple, perhaps because he honored humility and abhorred pride. He proved to be much more interested in how his followers related to others than in what they knew.

When I was a young adult, my Baptist church was in an unofficial competition with the Methodist church two blocks away. No one ever mentioned it, but the rivalry hung in the air like a murky fog whenever we interacted. For instance, when the Methodist church added a stunningly beautiful steeple to their church, the Baptist church added one at least three feet taller—and I've always wondered what Freud might have to say about that.

At one point, we Baptists hired a new but older pastor who had a well-worn doctoral degree. For several months, in spite of the fact that he insisted that everyone should call him "Brother Farley," every time he was introduced, 'Doctor' was emphasized one way or another. It seems we Baptists were very proud to have finally trumped the Methodists with a three-degree pastor.

Finally, in the most gracious reprimand I've ever witnessed, he addressed the problem from the pulpit, stating, "I've asked you over and over again to forget about calling me Dr. Farley and call me Brother Farley instead. I mean it. I don't want a doctoral degree ever separating me from anyone. We're all broken people. I'm broken too. I'm not a bit different from you. Besides, I need to tell you the truth about that degree. Those extra letters at the end of my name are just like the kink in a pig's tale. They're a real cute decoration, but they don't put any more meat on the pig."

Some of what we mistakenly believe is meat may very well be nothing more than greasy excess that weighs us down. For example, do you still remember the holy grail of sermon presentation? *Tell them what you are going to tell them; tell them; then tell them what you told them.* It's time to shed that advice. Unlearn it as soon as possible. And all those propositional sermons you were required to turn in to preaching professors, the ones with the carefully arranged and alliterated points? Those are already going the way of the dinosaur. Neither of these standard methods is proving to be effective for some very real reasons having to do with how our brains work. You will be reading much more on this in chapters 7 through 10.

This doesn't mean you won't be preaching. It does mean that your preaching will be avoiding the expressway and taking some much more interesting scenic routes. Nothing in this book negates the need for good preaching. God has always used preaching as the primary means to spread the news of his love for us. I suspect it always will be our most valuable professional tool. We will, however, need to add several more gizmos to our toolbox. Hopefully, this book will help you lay hold of some.

Cost #3: Plunder the Egyptians

In Exodus 3:21–22, as the Israelites were preparing to leave Egypt, God instructed them, "When you leave you will not go empty-handed. Every woman is to ask her neighbor and any woman living in her house for articles of silver and gold and for clothing, which you will put on your sons and daughters. And so you will plunder the Egyptians."

Irenaeus, Origen, Augustine, and John Wesley all used this powerful and memorable image to talk about God's sovereignty, explaining that because God is the creator of all good things, His people can use anything the world has to offer to bring glory to Him, especially the best the world has to offer. Moses' education in the schools of Egypt is one of the best examples of this. It was an integral part of the preparation that enabled him to be powerfully used by God to free the Israelite slaves.

The image of 'plundering the Egyptians' speaks to our tendency to label some things as *holy, sacred*, and *set apart,* while other things are permanently marked with a blistering branding iron as *secular, carnal,* and *worldly*. Everything God makes is holy––absolutely everything. We can choose to profane any of his gifts by using them to dishonor God, or we can opt to use those very same gifts to extend his love to the world. This includes so-called 'secular' knowledge.

For the purpose of becoming better teachers, plundering the Egyptians means we will be turning to the most recent findings of neuroscience and cognitive science. These disciplines are using new technologies to take a limited but very real peek inside the human brain––and that peek has been less like viewing the horizon through a pair of binoculars and more like watching an atom bomb detonate on the horizon. The mushrooming findings are sending shockwaves through halls of learning around the globe. I cannot claim the details are easy to understand, but fortunately I can say the resulting guidelines for teaching are not difficult to employ. You don't necessarily have to understand why an airplane stays in the air before you board it and find yourself soaring above the earth.

That said, I do not expect you to simply take my word that in 'doing this' or 'trying that' you will see your church grow in the grace and knowledge of Jesus Christ. You deserve more than the condescending opinions of yet another pretentious person sporting a decorative pigtail behind their name.

We will be delving into the realm of science, looking at a few key discoveries, and then asking how we can apply them as we attempt to lead our people to the throne of God. If you find yourself wading through some deeper water than you would like, remember that this is not an excursion for the sake of an intellectual workout. You are only wading ankle-deep through gray matter because it will give you a stable foundation on which to design worship, worship that can glorify God as it throws open safely-sealed doorways to the Spirit and introduces your congregation to new vistas of adoration.

So be forewarned––the remainder of this book will attempt to walk a fine line between describing how the mind works and suggesting practical ways you can put the information to use. Please forgive those times when you believe I've ended up too far to one side of that line. When you are passionately convinced of something, balance can be difficult to maintain.

A second warning needs to follow. These guidelines are in no way a 'formula' for worship. There are already too many cookie-cutter churches that rely more on imitating the latest flavor-of-the-month celebrity church than on the creative work of the Holy Spirit. Respected theologian and author Leonard Sweet observes, "It's easier to replicate than reproduce; to replicate a mass-produced program than to reproduce an original by intimate investigation of and investment in one's home ground—its seasons, flora, fauna, smells, sounds. We'd rather colonize the local than parent local color."[2]

Because the fresh breath of the Spirit is incapable of blowing a gust of stale air, spirit-led encounters with God are not duplicable. Moses' burning bush, Isaiah's vision of the throne room of heaven, and Gideon's fleece were all one-of-kind engagements with God. Our God-meetings too should be fresh, marked by a sense of discovery, grappled with rather than served up like identical fast-food hamburgers.

With this in mind, think of these guidelines less like a recipe for a specific food item and more like the stock ingredients that you always keep on hand in your kitchen—salt, pepper, eggs, flour, oil, milk, butter, and sugar. These simple ingredients can be combined in countless ways with other ingredients to create dishes as dissimilar as gumbo, chocolate cake, quiche, and chicken potpie.

The guidelines suggested here are simply stock components that can be mixed in creative ways with homegrown community, garden-fresh culture, and local faith tradition to create exceptional, artisanal worship experiences. Any example given is for the sake of demonstrating how the guidelines have been applied in a local situation. Used without discernment, an activity that helped generate changed lives in one church can be a disaster in another. Because each church is different, the way the methods are implemented must be different, customized to the local faith community. God has different plans for you and yours. He has already placed creative individuals in your church who can help

---

[2] Leonard Sweet, *The Greatest Story Never Told: Revive Us Again* (Nashville, TN: Abingdon Press, 2012), 72.

lead your congregation to do things of which no other church has ever dreamed. After giving thanks for those imaginative members, I suggest that you ask God to give you eyes to see exactly who they are.

The Pay-Off

The difference between enriching worship services using the insights of brain research as opposed to exclusively using more traditional methods of teaching can be the difference between teaching a follower of Jesus what to think and teaching a follower of Jesus how to think. It can be the difference between creating flexible, open-minded humans and rigid, know-it-all automatons. It can be the difference between a disciple whose brain is filled with memorized facts and a disciple who is filled with the Holy Spirit, who is starting to think and act in new ways—in Jesus ways. Considering the fact that the Church is in the transformation business, we cannot afford to ignore this valuable resource.

Chapter 2

FORGETTING TO REMEMBER

During my high school senior year, I was on the receiving end of a curse. No, it was not a four-letter word kind of curse; it was a four word kind of curse—a curse that bore unmistakable traces of dark magic. It all began with a competition that left me feeling a bit like a character from Suzanne Collins's series "The Hunger Games." Like the teenagers in her books, we just accepted this yearly ritual as a preordained part of adolescent life. No one questioned its appropriateness or its inevitability, nor did any of the competitors choose to play this game. We had to be chosen. Afterwards, our names were announced loudly over the crackling static of a loudspeaker system. During that much-anticipated announcement, our breathing would slow down and deepen because we knew that before the week had passed, the conscripted candidates would face each other in a public arena, one-on-one. By Friday, the victors would emerge amidst cheers with photographs following.

The name of our spirited but dispiriting game was actually quite innocuous, innocently called *Senior Class Who's Who*. The competition began when select seniors were nominated by the Student Council as the class's *Prettiest/Most Handsome, Most Athletic, Most Musical, Most Popular,* ad infinitum. Afterwards, the student body would cast ballots to choose their champions. Self-conscious losers would be left to lick invisible wounds. Like Snow White's wicked stepmother, no one wanted to be the second fairest in the land.

Surprisingly, the also-rans were not the only ones left with scars. Sometimes, the winners were the biggest losers of all. Imagine the thrill of being deemed *Prettiest* and then spending the rest of your life trying to live up to that title. Time and gravity alone guarantee that a day is coming when you will look less princess-pretty and more like a fairy-tale hag. Picture the elation of being named *Most Artistic* only to discover a decade later that no one values your work enough to pay you a living wage. Or just suppose you were christened *Most Likely to Succeed.* How many hours a week would you be willing to devote to proving that your peers got it right? Just who would you be willing to step on climbing the ladder to the top? This is why I call myself cursed. I was chosen to shoulder the impressive but highly intimidating title *Most Likely to Succeed.*

Already a perfectionist and an overachiever, this designation proved to be further motivation to drive myself onward, spurring me to perfect my perfectionism and to overachieve as an overachiever. Instead of choosing classes I could enjoy or even use, I enrolled in all the most difficult courses just to prove I could master the material. Physics? I sailed through it. Physiology? No sweat. Calculus? Who didn't need to know about rational functions, limits, and applications of derivatives?

As, it turns out I didn't. In all the years since I took those courses, I have never once had to figure out the convergence of an infinite sequence, the slope of a curve, or derive an equation for a projectile. There has been no occasion when I have found it necessary to balance a chemical equation or interpret research on how the body reacts to extreme temperatures, but with an unhealthy need to prove I was a worthy human being, I spent valuable time filling my head with a glut of unnecessary facts—useless particulars that I have never actually needed. Satisfied just to possess the head-knowledge, I felt prepared for anything (especially an appearance on *Jeopardy*).

The label affected me in yet another way—a more substantial way. Not only did I guzzle down gallons of information that would prove useless to me in later years, I missed out on things that could have added value to my life. In high school, I arrogantly assumed that anyone with a brain could learn to type, so I passed over typing for what I considered substantially heavier subject matter. I have regretted that decision ever since. As I sit here writing this, I am pecking away at my keyboard with little technique and no grace.

More regrettably, I was born with an artistic side that I needlessly neglected. As a child, nothing brought me more joy than drawing and painting. According to my teachers, I was gifted artistically. Ironically, those same teachers advised that art was not a viable major in college because it would never pay the bills. Painting might be a great hobby but, if I were to succeed in life, I needed a more practical profession.

I listened to my advisors and remained focused, enrolling in subjects that were more marketable, more left-brained. I never took another art class after seventh grade. It was only much later that I realized that doing so could have expanded my view of reality, given me a means to express my deepest thoughts, and offered a much-needed release from stress. Consequently, today I only play at what could have been a defining role in my life. Ironically, 'Miss Most Likely to Succeed" failed to succeed at developing her most natural and personally satisfying talent.

Note that I am not saying that physics, physiology, and calculus are useless disciplines—far from it. They are essential skills for almost every field of science. What I am saying is that there was a time in my life when I was so fixated on success that I made three big mistakes:

- I prided myself in what I knew intellectually.
- I knew more intellectually than I ever put into use.
- I did not pursue the things that would have actually enriched my life.

These same three mistakes can explain the cause of a major problem faced by the twenty-first century church, and if we are honest, we all know that we are facing a major problem.

We Pride Ourselves in What We Know

Because churches are composed of fallen humans, they are susceptible to every temptation known to humankind. One of the most enticing traps for the institutional church seems to be the bottomless pit of pride, especially pride in our particular brand of doctrine—in essence, pride in what we know. We have confused righteousness with being right. We have elevated head knowledge while neglecting heart knowledge.

Brain-Based Worship

In doing so, we have managed to distort the meanings of the words *faith* and *believe*. Many in today's church assume that to *have faith* or to *believe in the Lord Jesus Christ* means to give intellectual assent to the reality of the divine-human life of Jesus, his teachings, and his resurrection. Not so for the writers of Scripture.

When Paul invited the Philippian jailer to "Believe in the Lord Jesus . . ." he wasn't just calling him to intellectually accept a list of assertions about Jesus; he was challenging him to bet his life and the life of his family on the fact that Jesus was the Way (of love and compassion), the Truth (of God's revelation), and the Life (abundant and free).[1] The jailer was being summoned to follow in footsteps that were in direct opposition to what his culture dictated. Doing so could cost him his very life.

That type of commitment is a far cry from believing something as a fact. You can believe the fact that a low-fat diet is beneficial to your health even as you gorge on fries and a bacon double cheeseburger. You can be convinced that you need to start exercising regularly without ever taking the first step on the treadmill. You can believe that you need to stop smoking while lighting a Macanudo.

The faith the institutional church has proclaimed for more than two hundred years has been first and foremost a head thing, something that goes on in the less-than-three-pounds of gray matter located between the ears. When faith is reduced to the contents of one organ, although it may be easier to handle, it eventually leads to serious and undesirable side effects. Cerebral convictions grow and solidify over time, giving rise to severe swelling of the ego and hardening of the heart—a dangerous condition in which humans become convinced that they know more than they actually do. They may even grow to believe that they understand the God of creation simply because they have managed to whittle Him down to fit their opinions and prejudices.

A cerebral God is a God of certainty, not mystery—one who can be constrained to a pitifully small airtight container only slightly larger than a Tupperware cereal bowl. A cerebral God is also an idol. Those who worship these miniature versions of God can be so certain of their convictions that they attempt to impose their housebroken deity on

---
[1] Acts 16:31

others by broadcasting their wisdom in deeply divisive and bitingly critical ways from pulpits and over social media. They can be downright obnoxious in their certitude. Sadly, in settling for a cerebral God, they are trading the truth of God (God opposes the proud, but gives grace to the humble) for a lie (God loves me more than those who refuse to agree with what I know).[2]

And speaking of what we know, regular viewers of *The Tonight Show with Jay Leno* would anticipate with great relish his ongoing person-on-the-street segment *Jaywalking*. The concept was deliciously simple: While followed by a cameraman, Jay approached random people on the street and asked them to answer simple questions—very simple questions. In addition to its laugh-provoking potential, the segment had the exquisite secondary effect of making the viewer feel ever-so-much-more intelligent than the poor chumps Jay interviewed.

Some of the questions seemed almost impossible to get wrong, but one soon learns that the only thing that is really impossible is underestimating the general public. Many individuals drew blanks when asked questions such as "What is the filler material in a goose-down pillow?" or "What color is the White House?" We soon learned that common sense really isn't all that common.

In November of 1997 and in March of 2007, Jay elected to ask questions about Bible knowledge. Even the simplest queries baffled those being interviewed. A compilation of those answers would create a version of the Bible that looks something like this: *It all began "A long time ago in a galaxy far, far away..." On the first day of creation, God said, "Let there be peace." After God created Adam, he created Eve—either from an apple, the night sky, or a cow. Adam and Eve never had children. Cain and Abel were either close friends of Jesus or a sitcom (or possibly close friends of Jesus who had their own sit-com). Jesus himself was born almost 400 years ago. The Three Wise Men were obviously Hispanic because they were named Nina, Pinta, and Santa Maria. They brought the baby Jesus gifts of gold, frankincense, and wine. Because they supplied alcohol to a minor, they had to flee the country under the cover of darkness. When Jesus grew up, he became*

---

[2] 1 Peter 5:5

Brain-Based Worship

a carpenter, helped Noah build an ark, and then parted the Red Sea to let the ark get through.

No doubt, the five-minute clips were hilarious; they were also horrifying. They exposed a people who, having lost their biblical roots, are biding time on a crumbling foundation. With our foundational narratives eroding away, our collective gray matter is instead being filled with celebrity gossip, sports trivia, political indoctrination, and a storyline that convincingly teaches that the more we consume, the happier we will be. Even secular educators understand that a biblically illiterate public frankly lacks the necessary means to understand the numerous biblical allusions in historical records, great literature, and even popular music. Examples of those allusions include common phrases like *the patience of Job*, demanding someone's *head on a platter*, or thinking someone *walks on water*. They can include key pointers in literature (the names of characters in *Moby Dick*), and song lyrics as diverse as Dolly Parton's *Coat of Many Colors,* Coolio's *Gangsta Paradise* (*As I walk through the valley of the shadow of death . . .*), and Sting's *All This Time* (*Blessed are the poor, for they shall inherit the earth. Better to be poor than a fat man in the eye of a needle . . .*).

It's more than a little comforting for the Church to believe that the erosion of fundamental biblical knowledge is only happening out there in the world. It's also incorrect. Shortly after the first *Jaywalking* segment aired, a young adult group at the church I attended decided it would be fun to play a similar game at a class party. Confident that they would fare significantly better than those in the person-on-the-street interviews, they enthusiastically participated. Those who composed the questions kept them simple, but it soon became obvious that remedial Bible classes were needed.

In this group of eighteen frequent church attenders, no one could name more than seven of Jesus' twelve disciples, and several included Paul, Mark, and Luke in those they did name. Most could name no more than five of the Ten Commandments. Three could not name all four Gospels. When asked to name the occupation of specific characters, only a handful knew that Moses was a shepherd when he encountered the burning bush or that Andrew was a fisherman when Jesus invited him to be a follower. Only one knew that Paul supported himself as a tent-maker. When well-known passages were read aloud–the story of baby Moses in the bulrushes and the birth of the Church at Pentecost– few could identify the book from which the stories came. No one could put the following events in chronological order: birth of Jesus, birth of Moses, birth of David, birth of Abraham, birth of John the Baptist, birth of Samuel, and birth of Timothy. Though exposed to Scripture weekly, these young adults were shockingly unaware of the stories of individual characters or the overarching narrative of Scripture.

At another time, a young couple made an appointment to speak to me about a matter of importance. Dan and Tina were committed parents who worked with our teens. They never missed an opportunity to be in our worship services. They opened their home frequently to be used by the church for small-group studies. On this particular day, they were concerned about their six-year-old daughter, Emily. Emily had told them that God had spoken to her and told her she needed to be baptized.

Dan and Tina were convinced that Emily was too young to understand what God wanted. They were planning to refuse her request, but decided to seek counsel first. In the midst of our lengthy conversation that day, I said, "If you are uncomfortable, there is no need for you to make a final decision today. If God is speaking to Emily, he will continue to speak to her, and she will continue to talk to you about it. Don't forget that God had to speak to Samuel three times before he understood, and even then Eli had to help him understand that it was God speaking to him."

Dan looked slightly confused for a moment, but finally responded, "We haven't met Samuel or Eli yet. Can you introduce us so we can talk to them about their experience?"

Forget about the world being biblically illiterate; in too many cases, it's the Church that is biblically illiterate. We are rapidly losing touch with the very Scripture on which we base our faith. We do not know our own stories well enough to tell them to our children. Nor do we transmit those stories well during worship services.

Over the past three decades, it has become common to hear an entire sermon based on one verse instead of a complete passage of Scripture. While there may be no mention of the verse's context, there may be a full smorgasbord of unrelated verses used to back up the point the preacher is trying to make. The biblical story in which the verse appears may never be told, often because we preachers assume the audience already knows the story.

Instead of telling the story, we use razor-sharp rhetorical methods taught in our seminaries to serve up oratorical masterpieces replete with propositions, proposals, points, and plans. Our sermons are regularly couched in the terms of self-help––*Building a Christian Marriage, Raising Godly Children,* or *Five Steps to Powerful Prayer*––subtly conveying the message that the biblical passages must be supplemented because, alone, they do not offer the critical help we need to survive and thrive.

In the individual lives of our members, the situation is also disheartening. Even though there are those who habitually drink deeply from Scripture, many more do not. When they do sporadically read their Bibles, the most common technique used is the Ouija Board method– opening the Bible randomly, letting the eyes fall on a short passage, reading it without considering context, and then taking it as God's personal word for that moment. According to research conducted by Barna Group, the biggest problem facing the church today has less to do with people lacking a set of beliefs and more to do with having solidified beliefs "which they think are consistent with biblical teachings, and they are neither open to being proven wrong nor to learning new insights . . . By the time most Americans reach the age of 13 or 14, they think they pretty much know everything of value the Bible has to teach and they are no longer interested in learning more scriptural content."[3]

We Know More Than We Act On

In spite of the average churchgoer's conviction that they personally know God––what pleases God, what infuriates God, what makes God laugh with delight or cringe with loathing––they seem to have massive problems acting on that knowledge. Perhaps because of the strong belief

---

[3] Barna Group, "Barna Studies the Research: Offers a Year-in-Review Perspective," December 18, 2009. (acessed July 12,2013). http://www.barna.org/barna-update/article/12-faithspirituality/325-barna-studies-the-research-offers-a-year-in-review-perspective

that God saves by faith, not by works, many are able to rationalize away habitual inaction without too many mental gymnastics. Such twisted logic might sound something like this, "If I try too hard to follow in Jesus' footsteps, it might look like I'm trying to earn my salvation––and that would certainly offend God. Besides, God understands how busy my life is right now. He knows my resources are limited. And he knows that circumstances have changed drastically in 2000 years. He would never expect the same level of extreme faithfulness and trust in the rat race of the twenty-first century that he expected from heroes of the faith who lived in simpler times, would he?"

When those in our congregations do take some kind of action, it's often action that has been carefully planned and scheduled beforehand by a church staff person. When it comes to regularly and consistently feeding the hungry, visiting the prisoner, welcoming the stranger, forgiving the family member––daily living out the implications of the gospel in every relationship and in every situation––it's the exceptional Christian who lives this way, not the average Christian.

This begs the painful question: Are we being transformed into the image of Christ if our actions remain unchanged? In Matthew 21:28–32, Jesus told the story of a father who asked his two sons to come work with him in his vineyard. The first, with more important things to do, refused to come. The second son did not hesitate to consent to give his father assistance. He would have made any father proud in his eagerness to help––except for the fact that he never showed up. He never got his hands dirty or broke a sweat in the heat of the sun. The first brother, however, in spite of his negative answer, changed his mind after giving a little more thought to his father's request. He dropped what he was doing, and went straight to the field to work alongside his father. His words had been harsh, but his presence in the field made all the difference in the harvest.

After telling the story Jesus asked, "Which of the two did the will of his father?" In other words, "Weigh the evidence for yourself. Who actually acted in accordance to what the father wanted? What then was the critical factor when it came to pleasing the father?" Jesus understood that even though the notorious sinners surrounding him might have been getting all the words wrong, their lives had sometimes demonstrated genuine repentance and love. On the other hand, the lives of many highly religious people who said all the right things at all the right times, showed no evidence of such change.

When a person worships in spirit and in truth, when they give honor to a God who loves and blesses even those who do not return his love, when they give their heart to a God who cares for the downtrodden, when they stand in awe of a God who forgives, when they express devotion to a God who willingly sacrificed himself for their well-being, it changes who they are. It affects them inside and out. It's not just their thoughts that are transformed; their behavior is changed. Pride begins to melt away as they start to understand that they are no better and no worse than anyone else. Self-centered living becomes out of the question because their hearts are drawn to love the same people God loves. In due course, their actions begin to consistently flesh out their espoused beliefs, giving God exactly what Micah 6:8 tells us God requires. They "act justly, love mercy, and walk humbly with God"—not because they are checking off requirements on a legalistic checklist, but because that is the type of people they are becoming.

Worship that does not give rise to humility, mercy, and justice is simply not worship. Augustine poetically put it this way, "Hope has two beautiful daughters—their names are anger and courage; anger at the way things are, and courage to see that they do not remain the way they are." Long before Augustine wrote, a Chinese proverb advised, "Unless I act on what I know, I don't know even that."

If the lives of our people are not showing evidence of transformation, then we must ask ourselves how much genuine worship is actually happening. Are large parts of the congregation, perhaps including us, simply going through the motions of religious ritual? Do we worship on Sunday but continue to go about business as usual the rest of the week? Are we failing to connect with the fact that Christianity is not a system of intellectual belief? It is a challenge to live life in an entirely different way. Following Christ has got to be more than a religious veneer we glue over a life no different from anyone else's.

We Do Not Pursue the Things that Would Enrich Our Lives

In our misguided pursuit of knowledge about God (instead of a more intimate knowledge of God), we have traded our birthright for a bowl of pottage. In the erroneous belief that having faith means believing multiple propositions about God, we have managed to let the very things that could actually profit us most slip through the cracks.

For example, our seminaries have trained us to preach to a left-brained, logical world. We do this well—maybe too well. In the almost exclusive use of linear, propositional sermons, we are inadvertently overlooking an entire population of creative, imaginative, right-brained people. For centuries, both schools and churches have nurtured our linear thinkers while neglecting those whose brains operate more like pinball machines. How many of those overlooked people would love to contribute their oft-devalued gifts to the life of the Church if only asked? How much ability and talent is being squandered when we allow our right-brainers to sit on the sidelines? And if we believe that every member of the body of Christ has something to contribute to the well being of the faith community, are we exercising stewardship wisely?

Moreover, in emphasizing faith as an intellectual activity, we are unintentionally leading our parishioners down a dead-end road. How many leave worship services each week convinced that a head filled with all the right doctrine is the best Jesus has to offer? How many foolishly settle for the assurance that they will spend eternity in heaven while in the meantime they are missing out on the God possibilities that surround them right now? How many have never experienced the joy inherent in sacrificial generosity, the indescribable relief that accompanies forgiveness of an enemy, the self-confidence God bestows upon the person willing to turn the other cheek, the tranquility experienced in non-retaliation, the composed sense of personal integrity that comes from keeping a difficult promise no matter how large or small it may be? With the eager assistance of culture, too many professing Christians have been persuaded that although such virtues may have served well in a more primitive world, today they are unrealistic and idealistic.

When the Church distills faith to a brain activity, we subtly affirm this misguided belief.

Finally, in our love of knowledge, we have sacrificed transformation on the altar of information. God did not create us primarily to process information, propositions, points, and premises. He created us for relationships—wonderful, difficult, satisfying, painful, life-giving, heart-crushing, complicated relationships. Simply cramming a head already filled with too many facts with even more information will never bring about the type of transformation that leads to healthier relationships with God and others.

Transformation only begins when God gets hold of us in some kind of worship encounter. When he does, it always leads to changes in all other relationships. As we encounter God in worship, we become more aware of our own brokenness and, consequently, grow less judgmental about the brokenness of our neighbor. As he opens our eyes to personal blind spots, it becomes possible to look at others with compassion and empathy. Forgiving those who have wronged us becomes a real and appealing possibility. Wholehearted worship leads us to better grasp on reality, a more accurate understanding of self, and an acceptance of the fact that we actually are our brother's keeper.

Being transformed into the image of Jesus Christ is never an easy experience because it requires that we rethink our values, our priorities, and our passions in light of God's love for his creation. In doing so, we may find ourselves rejecting a consumeristic lifestyle, making reparations for injuries that we have caused, changing political or social positions, or taking the first step to reconcile with a family member or friend. Our thoughts and actions may begin to shift in ways that amaze us and alarm others, but through it all, God is transforming us, making us more loving people who are learning to live deliberately and abundantly.

Fervent worship is essential to becoming authentically human. So just why is it so difficult to find, and how can the Church recover it as an extraordinary but ordinary part of our ministry?

Chapter 3

Dismembered

The date on planet Earth was January 5, 1968, but in an alternative Trekkie universe, it was Stardate 3211.7. During a routine inspection of an unmanned station at Gamma II, Kirk, Uhura, and Chekov were captured and imprisoned by race of humanoids on the planet Triskelion. The humanoids were themselves slaves, oppressed and controlled by a group of reclusive and unseen planetary rulers called The Providers. The Providers forced the humanoids to do their will, using them for entertainment purposes in gladiator-style games of combat.

The crewmembers of the Enterprise were taken to holding cells, shackled to the walls, and fitted with metal collars that were engineered to deliver severe pain if they disobeyed their captors. There, they were informed that they would spend the rest of their lives as slaves whose only reason for existence was to accommodate The Providers' thirst for blood sport.

After a failed escape attempt, Kirk was transported to a seemingly deserted but expansive bunker buried deep beneath the surface of the planet. He cautiously made his way through the chamber to its center where, at long last, he met his nemeses face to face, the only problem being that The Providers had no faces. Instead of physical beings, Kirk met three disembodied, glowing brains that lived inside a dome-shaped structure. The brains explained telepathically that they were ancient beings who had evolved to the point that they no longer needed physical bodies, but without bodies they discovered that they were easily bored. As a remedy for their boredom, they enslaved droves of humanoids for entertainment purposes, waging bets over the outcome of fight-to-the-death gladiator contests between them.[1]

The disembodied brain made its first public appearance long before 1968. It had been a recurring TV and cinema character ever since 1942 when the movie *Donovan's Brain* started it all. The semi-human creature has since been featured in horror movies (*Fiend Without a Face*), comedies (*The Man With Two Brains*), cartoons (*Futurama*), role-playing games (*Dungeons and Dragons*), and video games (*Metroid*). In each instance, the cold, logical intelligence of a disembodied brain was viewed as more rational, more powerful, and occasionally even preferable to the standard brain-body arrangement.

Two *Star Trek* characters, Mr. Spock and Data, became paradigms for those attracted to the notion that it is advantageous to be capable of reasoning without the interference of a pesky human body and its accompanying emotional reactions. Because Spock's father was a normal green-blooded Vulcan, Spock inherited the biological ability to disregard feelings. Data, on the other hand, was a sentient android who offered viewers an outsider's perspective on the role of human emotions.

For researchers, logic is an irreplaceable tool that helps them determine why things are as they are. Emotional attachment to the outcome of a study is always unadvisable because it can affect the interpretation of research results. It has even caused some to falsify those results. Approximately two percent of researchers have admitted to such misconduct.[2] It is not surprising that those working in disciplines such as science, statistics, or mathematics might consider the ability to work from a position of pure logic an asset.

On the other hand, it is highly problematic to encounter followers of the Incarnate Christ who disdain the flesh-and-blood body. You might even call it 'most illogical.'

---

[1] *Star Trek*, "The Gamesters of Triskelion," episode no. 45, January 5, 1968.

[2] Daniele Fanelli, "How Many Scientists Fabricate and Falsify Research? A Systematic Review and Meta-Analysis of Survey Data," *PLOS ONE* September 24, 2009, http://www.plosone.org/article/info%3Adoi_%2F10.1371%2Fjournal.pone.0005738

Disembodied Bliss?

At the Council of Chalcedon (451 CE), Orthodox Christianity affirmed that Jesus, as the second person of the Trinity, became flesh. God somehow stepped through the wafer-thin membrane that separates the seen from the unseen, and when he did, he stepped into a human body. He honored the human body of Mary by stepping into her womb, where, for the first time since time began, the DNA of humanity fused with the very essence of God. In the flesh-and-blood body of Jesus, the divine nature of God united with human nature in one person who was "truly God and truly man." This fact alone should cause us to stand in awe of and to give thanks for the human body. Regrettably, that is not always the case.

I grew up in a Protestant church that taught me to imagine eternity with Christ as one long disembodied state of spiritual consciousness. Until that time arrived, while stuck with a physical body, I was to keep in mind that there was something hopelessly and incurably wrong with it. I was expected to look with loathing on my weak human flesh, always mistrusting what it most deeply sensed and felt.

In the meantime, I was to gain comfort in knowing that a glorious day was coming when I would finally leave a rotting corpse behind. The 'real me' would morph into an uncorrupted, incorporeal spiritual being—rather like that of *Star Trek*'s Providers. In the church that made me, 'no body' was equated with 'no temptation.' Accordingly, I walked through decades of my life believing that my own body was an impediment to following Jesus.

I was not alone. A long line of body-loathing predecessors littered earlier centuries, some of who carried contempt for their own bodies to almost unimaginable heights. Asceticism, a severe lifestyle in which all forms of indulgence and pleasure are avoided, grew from just such a mentality.

Convinced that the body is an obstacle to overcome, the ascetics tried to break it by punishing it. In fifth-century Syria, Simeon Stylites attempted to flee bodily pleasure by vowing to live in a space less than twenty meters in diameter. As more and more pilgrims sought him out for advice, he tried to escape them by living on a small platform, approximately one square meter in size, atop of a six foot-tall pillar. Over time, he extended the pillar to more than fifty feet tall and added a railing. There, he stayed until his death some thirty-seven years later.

In the fifteenth century, Thomas More, Lord Chancellor of England who served during the reign of Henry VIII, cozied up to agony by wearing a hair shirt under his outer attire. The earliest hair shirts were made of coarse animal fur that irritated the skin. By More's time, it was common to weave additional items such as twigs or wire into the garment, thus ensuring the body would never experience a single moment of carnal pleasure. In 1669, Puritan Thomas Watson penned, "The flesh is a bosom traitor; it is like the Trojan horse within the walls, which does all the mischief. The flesh is a sly enemy—it kills by embracing. . . . The flesh, by its soft embraces, sucks out of the heart all good." On the far extreme of extremism were those such as the Los Hermanos Penitentes, a nineteenth-century semi-secret society of flagellants among the Roman Catholics of Colorado and New Mexico.

Few in today's American church are even slightly tempted to enter the bizarre realm of self-punishment, but that does not mean that the Church has entirely embraced the human body as a good creation of God. Even though she may give lip service to the idea, in practice, the Church can still deny the gift of embodiment in the way we preach and in the way we conduct worship.

How does our unconscious rejection of the body manifest itself during twenty-first-century worship? Is there a mysterious connection between the way we understand the relationship between body and mind and the breakdown of effective discipleship within the church—a connection that until recently has totally escaped our awareness? How would a different understanding of the mind-body connection affect our teaching?

With these questions in mind, let us embark on a short history of a series of unfortunate events that landed us in the middle of decline and disinterest in the greatest story ever told.

Paula Champion-Jones

The Art of Dismembering Humans

To *dismember* something is to pull it apart, to cut it into smaller pieces, to deprive it of its original unity, to mutilate it. In the words of Leonard Sweet, "To dissect something is to kill it." Our view of who we are as humans has been slowly and systematically dismembered as we have dissected Homo sapiens in all manners of ways. But dissect them we do—detaching head from heart, slicing intellect from emotion, unfastening spirit from body, or splitting the soul from the destined-to-decay corpse.

Although the dismemberment of mind from body might appear to be a relatively new cinematic phenomenon, the emergence of a disembodied view of intelligence can be traced back at least to the ideas of seventeenth-century philosopher René Descartes. Descartes alleged that the human body works like a machine controlled by the laws of nature. At the same time, he thought the mind was nonmaterial, and thus not limited by those same laws. Descartes explained that although the mind controlled the body, the easily swayed and overly emotional body could also influence the mind, causing the otherwise rational mind to act irrationally. His bottom line belief was that being human has nothing to do with having a body and everything to do with having a brain. His concept of an immaterial, logical, unpolluted mind trapped inside a mechanical, emotional, illogical body became known as *dualism*. Dualism seduced the Western world into believing that the human body is a handicap, an instrument of interference that only gets in the way of objectivity and hard-edged logic. This mistaken belief continues to affect us today, leading many to insist that human reason is hopelessly contaminated by emotion.

It's not a coincidence that at around the same time the disembodied brain began to make its appearance on the big screen, behaviorism and operant conditioning made their appearance in the classroom, promptly becoming the most widely accepted models for educators. Those adopting the behaviorist model believed that all behavior could be explained scientifically without taking mental and emotional states into consideration. By the mid-twentieth century, with every student in Psychology 101 introduced to Pavlov's salivating dogs, learning was considered to be nothing more or less than a change in behavior brought on by reflexive responses to stimuli.

Thankfully, some questioned this valuable but simplistic theory of learning, arguing that it implied you could finesse a person into learning or doing anything with enough reward or punishment. Moreover, educators who relied predominately on operant conditioning were unintentionally creating passive learners whose so-called mechanical bodies simply followed along behind their skillfully manipulated brains, suggesting that there was very little difference between humans and Pavlov's animals.

In 1963, a new philosophy of learning, *reception learning*, dehumanized the learner even further as it spread the idea that the brain is nothing more than a container into which information prepared by a teacher is conveniently poured. According to this theory, people do not 'discover' knowledge; knowledge is given to them. The teacher's task consisted of preparing the needed knowledge by organizing it in a linear way, imposing an interpretation on the knowledge, and finally transferring it directly to the learner. Because the lecture method was heralded as the highest form of teaching, talking heads that dished out what they thought the public needed to know became the norm.

Both theories (behaviorism and reception learning) have had some positive impact on instruction. Both have also been detrimental as well, making it acceptable for well-meaning teachers to lecture away while students passively received the benefit of the instructor's scholarship and later regurgitated robot-like knowledge.

Teaching is about so much more than drilling concepts into brains, yet for too long we have accepted this as the norm. No doubt, you have sat in classrooms and sanctuary situations where the teaching was highly structured, linear, and did not allow you to actively engage with either the subject matter or the teacher. Do you remember those experiences fondly? How many of those lectures can you in fact even remember? How much impact did observing someone orate have on your life? Did you actually look forward to sitting on a hard desk or pew for an hour or so while listening to someone make a presentation? Were you so enthusiastic about what you learned that you couldn't wait to put your new knowledge into practice?

If you are like most people, you were more likely strongly and permanently affected on those occasions when you were invited to get your hands dirty while learning, when you worked in a simulated situation or an unfamiliar arena, when you discovered a concept for yourself, or when you had some degree of say-so in what you would study.

Notable educators have been calling for a move away from the lecture method since the turn of the twentieth century when John Dewey championed 'progressive education.' Dewey advocated for experiential learning-by-doing. Every lecture was always to be supplemented with some form of student involvement with the subject. At the same time, Marie Montessori was developing schools in which young students were given the independence to choose activities from a prescribed range of options. Throughout history, the best teachers (including Jesus) have intuitively taught without depending solely on lecture. In addition to discourse, they also actively involved students with subject matter and encouraged individual preferences and choices. The good news is that due to recent findings in neuroscience, their seemingly unorthodox methods are being vindicated over and over again.

Doing Business With Descartes

Predictably, the same educational models that have structured public education are also prevalent in our churches. It has been said that we teach as we were taught; nowhere does this hold truer than in Christian churches. The mainstay of the twenty-first-century worship service is the sermon—a rhetorical lecture delivered in a linear sequence with no diverging path. Sermons tend toward left-brain lectures that focus on checklists of what to believe intellectually or do's and don'ts directed predominately at outward behavior and appearance.

With correct knowledge and behavior emphasized, the capacity to unquestionably agree with official church doctrine is more highly valued than the ability to think. In some churches, the pastor is completely comfortable thinking for the membership, telling them what to believe, what is (or is not) acceptable, how to interpret Scripture, even how to vote. At times, having been led to believe that their congregations need simplistic, easily digested sermons, the preacher attempts to introduce, delve into, and even wrap up a difficult subject in three or four pithy points before tying it up with a glittery bow twenty minutes later. The worshipers are expected to receive, retain, and act on that information with little or no input. The pastor would be shocked beyond belief if someone dared to raise a hand in the middle of the sermon, hoping to ask a question or to contribute personal insight to the subject.

If we are honest with ourselves, we must admit that we are most comfortable when congregational participation is limited to singing a few pre-selected songs, reading through a printed liturgy, and sitting or standing on cue. We assume that if our listeners have managed to stay awake throughout the service that learning and transformation have occurred. This begs the question, "Has it really?"

Ironic isn't it? In spite of the facts that for going on three centuries the Church has emphasized head knowledge, and that today roughly 338,000 local Christian churches in the U.S. conduct at least one worship service each week, the American church has essentially raised a biblically illiterate generation.[3] It may be painful for us to admit, but the traditional worship service structured around a sermon built on rhetoric and bolstered by logic is no longer working. To put it bluntly, few people ever remember our sermons or services. Fewer still act on them.

We are presently investing countless words in our attempt to generate disciples for The Living Word, but our word-heavy investment is not paying off in transformed lives. In addressing our failure to make disciples, Dallas Willard asks the Church to examine herself. "Should we not at least consider the possibility that this poor result is not in spite of what we teach and how we teach, but precisely because of it? Might that not lead to our discerning why the power of Jesus and his gospel has been cut off from ordinary human existence, leaving it adrift from the flow of his eternal kind of life?"[4]

---

[3] Hartford Institute for Religion Research, *"Fast Facts about American Religion,"* (Hartford Seminary: Hartford, CT, 2012), http://hirr.hartsem.edu/research/fastfacts/fast_facts.html (accessed June 19, 2013).

[4] Dallas Willard, *The Divine Conspiracy* (San Francisco: HarperSanFrancisco, 1998), 40.

According to church futurist Leonard Sweet, "Religious learning systems must be based on new academic paradigms that shift from passive learning modes to active learning modes, especially ones where students learn habits of mind and habits of the soul at their own rate and in their own area of special interest."[5]

Just what are these 'new academic paradigms' that have the potential to reshape the future of the church? Might they offer us the necessary tools to design more powerful worship? Could they move the sermon to a new level of effectiveness? Is there a possibility that if we are willing to step out of our comfort zone and change the way we conduct worship that it might result in more passionate followers of Jesus Christ, followers who are being transformed into his perfect image? And of utmost importance, can these methods be utilized with integrity during a service designed to honor our God?

---

[5] Leonard Sweet, *11 Genetic Gateways to Spiritual Awakening* (Nashville: Abingdon Press, 1998), 6.

Chapter 4

DESIGNED TO RE-MEMBER

Shortly after our oldest daughter turned three, she verbalized what to her was an entirely logical understanding of the way the human body operates. We were seated at the table for lunch when the phone rang—and there actually was a time BC (before cells) when there was a single telephone in each house permanently positioned in one location. I left the room for a few moments to answer the beckoning ring. Upon returning, I found Rachel standing up in her chair in what can only be described as a bizarrely twisted position. Her body was technically facing the table, but her torso tilted drastically to the rear as if she were attempting a backbend. Her blonde ringlets draped over the back of her chair as she gripped the tabletop with her left hand, holding on for dear life to prevent her chair from overturning. With her right hand she was depositing one lima bean at a time into her gaping mouth, then chewing it and swallowing.

As my normally no-nonsense daughter persisted in her avant-garde dining demonstration, I paused in the doorway, watching her munching away in all her contorted glory. Finally unable to contain my curiosity any longer I asked, "Rachel, what *are* you doing?" She responded with, what to her, was a perfectly obvious and entirely rational answer. "Yesterday, I swallowed all my food down so my legs will grow faster. Today, I'm swallowing all my food up so my hair will grow faster."

Until recently, our theories concerning human learning were only slightly more sophisticated than Rachel's theory about hair growth. The majority of those theories have endorsed the idea that humans are rational beings whose logical mental abilities are severely compromised by their emotional bodies. As a result, both academia and religious institutions have virtually ignored the body, convinced that it has no role in thought. Until recently there has been no way to gather hard data to prove or disprove otherwise. We could only make educated guesses about the 'hows' and 'whys' of learning.

During the closing decades of the twentieth century, that changed. Sophisticated technologies were developed that would finally allow serious investigation of the learning process. Today, testing methods such as functional magnetic resonance imaging (fMRI), electroencephalography (EEG), and computer-assisted tomography (CAT) are drawing back the curtain on the concealed workings of the human mind. As a result, the discipline of cognitive neuroscience is flourishing.

Admittedly, cognitive neuroscience is in its infancy. Even though it has already shed fresh light on an area that has long been cloaked in darkness, there is much still to be learned about the workings of the brain. Commenting on the unfolding nature of all scientific knowledge, science, technology, and culture writer David DiSalvo reminds us, "The business of science is not to provide us with settled answers that we can comfortably rest our heads upon at night. Indeed, we are wise to expect more new questions than answers from any research campaign worth discussing."[1]

Benjamin Bergen, a University of California professor of cognitive science, enthusiastically declares, "This is the age of cognitive science. Had we been born earlier, we might be exploring new continents. Born later, we might be gallivanting through the stars. But right now, at this time in our history, the vast, tantalizing expanse that begs to be discovered is the human mind."[2]

Recent exploration of this new frontier has resulted in an explosion of previously unavailable information from which a new paradigm for teaching has developed. Known as *brain-based learning,* it is offering

---

[1] David DiSalvo, *What Makes Your Brain Happy and Why You Should Do the Opposite* (New York: Prometheus Books, 2011), 22.

[2] Benjamin K. Bergen, *Louder Than Words: The New Science of How the Mind Makes Meaning* (New York: Basic Books, 2012), 5.

deeper insight into how the teacher can create the right conditions for transformational learning. Those who employ brain-based teaching strive to design brain-friendly learning environments that cooperate with the brain, that joins forces with it in such a way that the brain is empowered to learn as it was originally designed it learn.

Reunited, And It Feels So Good

Contrary to Descartes' belief that the brain exists separately from the body, we now know that body and brain are intimately connected. Our bodies are not containers for who we are. Our bodies are who we are— and we are not cold-blooded thinking machines. We are sensory-motor-emotional-thinking beings. Our body and brain exist in an indissoluble symbiotic relationship.

The body informs the brain just as the brain informs the body. Renowned cognitive linguist George Lakoff writes in his introduction to Benjamin Bergen's *Louder Than Words*, "Every thought we have or can have, every goal we set, every decision or judgment we make, every idea we communicate makes use of the same embodied system we use to perceive, act, and feel. None of it is abstract in any way. Not moral systems. Not political ideologies. Not mathematics or scientific theories. And not language."[3] Our bodies affect every aspect of our thought, reason, and behavior.

In a nutshell, brain-based learning theory proposes that we humans are astoundingly competent learning machines. From the day we are born, we are designed to take in and make meaning of information so effectively that we normally never even think about it. Ninety-nine percent of what we learn, we learn unconsciously as our mind skillfully processes, detects, and deals with an endless bombardment of sensory information—sights, sounds, language, text, smells, tactile sensations, and more. Only one percent of what we know was learned while sitting in a traditional class, lecture, or sermon. All the rest, and most of the best, we learned effortlessly as our mind and body worked together to make meaning out of the circumstances and sensations of our life.

---

[3] Bergen, *Louder Than Words*, 5.

More comprehensive and holistic than any earlier learning theory, brain-based learning theory reunites, or re-members, the mind and body that dualism once dismembered. We now know beyond a doubt that there is no division between the body and brain. None. Therefore, the most effective way to empower the mind is to involve the body.

Any teacher who wants to activate both body and mind for learning needs to be familiar with a few of the findings of brain science and the implications of those findings for learning. We will begin with the two biggies that form the foundation upon which everything else is built.

Meaning Making and Survival

Of everything your mind does apart from spurring your heart to beat and your lungs to take in air, making meaning is the most important. The brain craves meaning like a Kardashian craves attention. Why?

The main task of the brain is to tune in to anything that can help you survive—physically or emotionally—so your very biology drives you to seek out any and all information leading to that end. Moment by moment, the brain is simultaneously scanning the distant horizon while examining your immediate surroundings, always on the alert for approaching danger even as you go through your daily routine. Designed for survival purposes, your brain is at its best when it is informally taking in information through your senses in a comparatively chaotic manner. In fact, you were never designed to learn on demand or to learn linear, propositional facts in a formal classroom situation.[4] Traditional classroom practices can even impede learning.

Yes. You read that right. Traditional classroom practices can actually hinder learning. All those lectures you sat through, all those notes you took, all those lists you memorized? It's not that they did you any harm.

---

[4] Propositional knowledge is knowledge received as a statement, usually in a lecture. The statement can be characterized as either true or false. An example would be, "There are five types of prayer." Propositional knowledge is in contrast to procedural knowledge (knowing how to do something, such as drive) and personal knowledge (knowledge by acquaintance, such as knowing a city). Having propositional knowledge about something is not enough to produce either personal knowledge or procedural knowledge.

There is just a much more effective (and fun) way to learn—a way that leaves you wanting to learn more.

And we humans always want to learn more. As a matter of fact, we can't help wanting to learn more. Our survival depends on what we learn about our environment from one second to the next. Because survival is always the highest thing on our priority list, we are on nonstop alert for any and all information that might contribute to our survival. There is never a time when we are *not* motivated to learn. We couldn't stop learning, even if we wanted to.

God fashioned us in such a way that our central control center (the brain) is thoroughly linked to a vast network of other nerve cells running throughout the entire body. The various components of our nervous system vigilantly communicate with each other, signaling each other of danger twenty-four hours a day—even as we sleep. When we hear a strange bump in the night, we react with more than just our hearing ears. We react with our entire body by instinctively jumping. Our pulse grows rapid. Our heart begins to pound. Our breathing becomes faster and shallower. Our mind kicks into overdrive as it formulates possible explanations. This all happens in a fraction of a second because a rapid response to what our senses detect can mean the difference between life and death.

On a constant quest to make sense out of the ten thousand things happening around us every moment, our mind constructs mental maps of reality by tirelessly working to take in countless, disconnected bits and pieces of information and discover patterns within them. Especially attracted to novelty and challenge because both can indicate danger, the mind pays close attention to them. Unexpected sounds, strange movements, out-of-place objects, or out-of-the-ordinary experiences all grab our attention.

If, for example, while driving home one night, you suddenly see flashing blue lights in the distance, without consciously thinking about it you will respond, probably by taking your foot off the gas and momentarily slowing down. Before your mind can deal with what it already knows (speed limit, road construction, whether or not you have warrants out for your arrest), your body reacts. As it does, the new information (police car ahead) is being examined, organized and integrated with existing knowledge. If that existing knowledge includes the facts that you are not speeding, that you are not in a construction zone, and that you are not wanted by the law, you will likely put your foot back on the gas and continue on your way. On the other hand, if an encounter with law enforcement could be threatening to you in any way, you may chose to slow down even more (or even take the next turn).

If the brain can make a connection between new material and what is already known, that new material is even more relevant, and therefore, more memorable. In the above example, if shortly before you saw the flashing blue lights you heard a radio announcement about a manhunt for a dangerous escaped convict in the area, because *manhunt*, *convict*, and *flashing police lights* are effortlessly linked mentally, it is likely that you will remember this experience a year later. If, however, the radio station never made such an announcement, you would quickly forget the whole thing.

We can only deal with the never-ceasing flood of sensory information because the brain is an expert at selectively blocking out irrelevant information. It does this so it can give attention to the more important bits of data. For example, if you come face-to-face with a large bear while hiking in the woods, you will probably cease to hear the nearby lilting birdsong or the soothing sound of a rushing stream because any threat to your survival always has priority.

A humorous and well-known example of this kind of selective attention can be found on YouTube. Before watching a video clip of two teams passing a basketball around, the viewer is asked to count how many times the team members dressed in white uniforms pass the ball. About thirty seconds into the one-minute, twenty-two second video clip, a person in a gorilla suit wanders across the court while looking directly at the camera. Before strolling out of sight, he even thumps his chest for good measure, but half the viewers who are focusing intently on counting the number of times the white team passes the ball, never even notice the gorilla.[5] If your priority is counting ball passes, even big, hairy issues can be unimportant.

---

[5] Daniel Simons, Christopher Chabris, "Selective Attention Test," (Champaign, IL: Viscog Productions, 1999), http://www.youtube.com/watch?v=vJG698U2Mvo.

Unrelated information actually does harm, not because it distracts us, but because it hinders pattern formation. If we don't see where information fits, our already overworked mind can be thrown into confusion. That's why we all hate sitting through a lecture where the speaker is metaphorically chasing rabbits and heading down side trails. Because our mind has enough to handle without being littered with irrelevant debris, it rebels in irritation.

We can be so intent on seeking meaning and patterns in everything that we even find them where none exists. This explains reports of finding an image of Jesus on a grilled-cheese sandwich or seeing a cloud formation that looks like a dragon. I once lived in a house in which the bath was partially paneled. Next to the closet, in the grain of the wood paneling, was a six-inch wood whirl that looked for all the world like a cartoon image of Satan's head––pointed goatee, curved horns, scowling eyes. I never mentioned it to anyone because I knew how superstitious some of my family members could be. One would have insisted on remodeling the bath, performing an exorcism, or both.

This same compulsion to look for patterns explains why some people, in their sincere attempts to figure something out, can jump to absurd conclusions. One particularly hot and dry Alabama summer, we visited my husband's grandmother. She had always taken a great deal of pride in her garden, so we expected a vegetable-laden table whenever we visited. Not so that year. She apologized for what to her was a meager meal, and then talked at length about the three-month long drought. Seemingly forgetting that she lived near a military airbase, she told us that she had repeatedly seen airplanes flying over her home. Those same plans had regularly flown over for decades, but she was now convinced that the government was conducting secret experiments in the area, seeding the clouds with something that was "drying them up." Blaming the party in-office at the time, she vowed to vote them out come November. Nonsense? Definitely. But we have all jumped to equally incorrect conclusions when our minds were searching for explanations.

Parallel Processing

The brain is a parallel processor that has the ability to function on many levels at once—always with the goal of making meaning from the sensory input it gathers. It spends its days (and nights) miraculously carrying out multiple operations, processing input from several different sources simultaneously. If this were not happening, it would be impossible to see while we were listening to someone, or taste while we were touching something. Even more complicated, the brain is carrying out multiple operations as it processes information from just one sense. We do not simply 'see' a bird. Based on that seeing, our mind simultaneously processes and analyzes the shape, color, depth, and motion of the bird.

As the brain does all this, it is also comparing the newly received visual information to the stored memories of everything else that it has ever processed. It immediately classifies what you are seeing as animal, not mineral, and as bird, not mammal or fish. The same complicated process happens with all our senses. For example, when we hear something, our brain is making numerous judgments about the sound. How loud is it? From what direction is it coming? How far away is it? Is the pitch high or low? Is the sound melodic or discordant? Threatening or pleasant? Even though you may have no idea what the words *timbre* or *phase* mean in connection to hearing, your brain is also making judgments about those qualities.

As the brain processes new information from one sense, it does so without shutting down the processing of information from the other senses unless under some kind of extreme threat (remember the bear in the woods). Even while focusing as intently as possible on the above-mentioned bird, we will still hear a car backfire. We will still be aware of the sensation of rain if it begins to fall on our face. We will still smell the wet dog standing beside us.

This seamless processing of new sensory input with stored memories miraculously goes on all day, every day, in every imaginable situation. Designed by God to carry out numerous operations at once, the brain is the ultimate multitasker. It is at its best while processing data coming from several sources at once—if the incoming data all relates to the same subject.

As a toddler randomly flips back and forth through the pages of *Mother Goose Rhymes* while listening to a recording of *Old MacDonald Had a Farm,* waving at her dog, imitating the sounds of a various farm animals, drinking milk, and eating a scrambled egg for breakfast, she is learning through all her senses simultaneously. A teen who is surfing the Internet to research a political-science assignment while simultaneously listening to the evening news, browsing through a newspaper for related articles, and talking on his cell to a friend about said assignment––and still moving with ease from one web site to the next with no particular strategy in mind––is learning.

Yet, many with teaching responsibilities have been taught to address only one sense at a time––usually hearing or sight. The idea of a student multitasking while learning is practically heretical. Brain science is proving the fallacy of this stance. As long as the individual components of the multi-tasking are related to each other, they interact and build on each other. The best teachers intentionally employ diverse sensory stimulation and offer several different ways to learn the same information.

Learning consultants Renata Numela Caine and Geoffrey Caine are convinced that no single method of teaching is ever sufficient to address the wide variations in the human mind. The teacher must design learning situations that address different learning styles. Such design would offer multiple ways to process the same information while being flexible enough to meet the needs of the group, the individual, and even the classroom itself. The design works even better when it includes collaborative learning, discovery learning, or incorporates musical connections.

Rather than teach in a linear fashion, the best teachers organize and choreograph learning. The Caines state, "Like the brain, good teaching should 'orchestrate' all the dimensions of parallel processing . . . . Teachers need a frame of reference that enables them to select from the vast array of methods and approaches that are available."[6] Expect to see more on this throughout the remainder of this book.

---

[6] Renata Nummela Caine and Geoffrey Caine, "Understanding a Brain-Based Approach to Learning and Teaching," *Educational Leadership* 48, no. 2 (October 1990), 66, accessed October 18, 2011, http://www.ascd.org/ASCD/pdf/journals/ed_lead/el199010caine.pdf.

Chapter 5

MENACES TO MEMORY

The sanctuary was thoroughly modern and elegantly understated. Its furnishings were aesthetically striking, bordering on minimalist. Beneath the soaring ceiling, the stage and chairs were fashioned from blonde wood crafted in the clean, simple lines of Scandinavian design. Surrounded by those chairs on three sides, the low stage stretched forward into the spacious room. Well-shaped arched windows, each of which boasted perfectly clear panes that sparkled like diamonds in the morning sun, complimented the watery-green walls.

The sanctuary was marked by an unusual air of tranquility that invited reverence and prayer––unless you happened to be there between the hours of 9 a.m. and noon. During those morning hours, it only invited headaches. Since sanctuaries are most frequently used during the morning hours, this presented a problem of megalithic proportions.

In designing the building, no one had anticipated one major complication that would come with building this particular plan on top of a tall hill that overlooked the community. With entirely nothing between the worshiper and the outside world but clear, crystalline panes of glass, during the morning hours the sunlight poured in completely unobstructed. Anyone sitting on the right side of the room was exposed to a blinding, full-frontal, headache producing view of Old Sol.

The gray skies of winter made the brightness somewhat more bearable, but summer months were particularly difficult. Bright, beautiful days intensified the discomfort as the already potent rays reflected off windshields and bumpers in the parking lot. The unyielding light, magnified to the nth degree, caused people to squint through entire worship services. It took only a couple of weeks for some in the congregation to migrate permanently to the left side of the sanctuary, but even those who weren't facing the sun still squinted in their attempt to see the carefully chosen words and images projected onto the sizeable and expensive overhead screen—utterly washed-out in the sun-drenched room.

I loved that church dearly, but weekly facing that wall of light was something I grew to dread. Wired in such a way that I never get a headache unless I am facing a bright light for an extended period of time, I have lived my life avoiding powerful stage lights, sun-bathed beaches, and glaring white snow. Some people may live for those very things, but blinding white is not my favorite color. In large doses it poses a threat to my state of well-being.

In that church, I discovered I was not alone. Others reacted to the intense optic overstimulation the same way as I—and no, they did not go into the new building hunting for something to complain about. Our spirits were high as we moved from a rented facility to a permanent home, but when it came to settling in to what at times felt like the interior of a carbon arc searchlight, the enthusiasm waned somewhat.

I'm sure you've heard the saying before, "If Mama ain't happy, ain't nobody happy." It can be paraphrased. "If the body ain't happy, ain't nothing else happy either." When the human body is uncomfortable—experiencing pain, distress, or irritation—the mind and spirit are also uncomfortable, experiencing their own type of distress. The reverse is also true. If you are in emotional distress, your body will react physically. Short-term emotional stress causes heart rate and breathing to increase as digestive activities decrease. Prolonged emotional stress can result in headaches, high blood pressure, heart problems, diabetes, skin conditions, asthma, arthritis, depression, and anxiety.

The human brain of 2013 A.D. is not enormously different from the human brain of 2013 B.C.E. Then, as now, we are primarily motivated to survive. We are born with a natural mechanism that constantly evaluates our surroundings and assesses threat levels. Am I about to be eaten by a predator? Is my clan about to be pillaged? With the prolonged drought, will the crops grow? Will I starve? Is the situation I find myself in good or bad? When the boss says, "We need to talk," am I about to be fired? Is that car following me? Am I dressed appropriately for this group? Do I need to escape this environment, or is it safe to get even closer? Our default is always set in the self-protective position.

When Is a Threat a Threat?

Repeatedly, when groups of people are asked to name their greatest fear, public speaking comes in first place. Death is a close second. Consequently, it has been said that while at a funeral, most people would rather be the body in the casket than the person giving the eulogy.

Surprisingly, I have no fear of public speaking. In first grade, my teacher required that we recite a poem or a passage of our choice in front of the class every Friday morning. My father, believing academics were a form of competition more admirable than football, chose my recitations for me——and he chose to 'win.' At seven years old, I was reciting *The Gettysburg Address, The Preamble to the Constitution*, and *Ode to a Grecian Urn* while my classmates recited *Hickory-Dickory-Dock*. I must admit that I envied them. Yes, Daddy was a little insane, but like most young children, I lived for his approval, so I cooperated and was highly praised for my effort. As a result, I've never been intimidated by the prospect of speaking in public.

On the other hand, if a spider of any size, color, genus, or species comes near me, my mind and body turn to Jell-O. Even if the spider is nowhere near me, if I am aware that one is in residence, I am uncomfortable. Why? Around the same time I was learning to recite historical documents, I had a serious run-in with a vengeful octomonster.

While I was playing under my grandmother's back porch, an enormous brown spider strolled across my path. Having bravely faced and killed the evil creatures before, I didn't hesitate to plop my foot right down on top of her——and regrettably, the spider was a her. She was carrying a swollen egg sack that, upon sudden compression, exploded under the pressure. Hundreds of baby spiders were sent scurrying in every direction. Some, obviously seeking retaliation, ran straight up my flip-flopped foot. I found myself screaming and slapping at my legs while my brother laughed as if he were watching an episode of *The Three Stooges.*

Ever since that encounter, I have been afraid of spiders. Intellectually, I know that there are only two poisonous species in my area. I also know exactly what they look like. I know that ninety-nine out of one hundred spiders I might encounter are not poisonous, but intellect has nothing to do with my primal gut-level reaction to arachnoids. In those moments, my brain is still seven years old, and spiders are a very real threat. If one sauntered across the pulpit while I was preaching, I'm honestly not sure that I could restrain a squeal while leaping from the stage.

Threats come in all shapes and sizes. Some are real. Some are imagined. An imagined threat is, nevertheless, a threat. We all have embarrassingly eccentric fears that set off raging internal alarms. Most of those fears are rooted in subjective experiences that have little to do with life or death situations, but even when an imaginary danger trips our body's alarm system, we go into autopilot.

Bottom line? Our brain reacts to an imagined threat exactly the same way it reacts to a real threat. Our so-called logical, objective brain is hijacked and propelled into a state of hyper-arousal. Our metabolic rate increases, as does perspiration to prevent overheating. Our adrenal cortex produces cortisol to keep our blood sugar and blood pressure high so we can have the energy to either make a hasty retreat or run straight into the mouth of the dragon. For the same reason, blood flow to every other organ decreases so blood flow to muscles can increase. All non-essential functions completely stop. Our body even stops digesting food so more energy is available to protect us from harm––and that explains why so many people have digestive problems when under stress. Most importantly, the decreased blood flow to the brain causes all higher-order thinking to cease and desist.

We don't even have to consciously know that we feel threatened for all of those responses to kick into play. At times, we may experience an unexplained inner turmoil, a subjectively unpleasant feeling of impending doom. Commonly known as *anxiety,* this is the brain's reaction to an unrecognized, unspecific threat. The person suffering anxiety is in a state of prolonged fear. They experience all the same symptoms as a person facing an immediate threat––restlessness, inability to concentrate, digestive problems, and muscular tension. With optimal energy directed toward survival, little is left for more critical thinking.

I once heard a woman describe living with anxiety by saying, "Sometimes I feel like a goldfish. I'm fed. My water is changed regularly. My home is carpeted with colorful gravel and furnished with nice green plants. I even have a lovely little castle. Every single one of my needs is taken care of. I should be happy. It's just that I feel like the tank that I'm living in is really a food processor, and I'm just waiting for someone to push *puree*."

Brain-based-learning pioneer Eric Jensen states that anytime a person feels threatened, the brain "loses its ability to correctly interpret subtle clues from the environment . . . loses some of its ability to store, index, and access information . . . loses some of its ability to perceive relationships and patterns . . . and is less able to use higher-order thinking skills."[1] The act of learning is severely impeded anytime the learner feels that safety is threatened by a real or imagined, physical or emotional danger. Any type of sensed threat makes it more difficult to absorb new information or adopt new behavior.

The good news is that if the learner feels that they are in a safe learning environment, all stress does not have to be eliminated. A measured level of stress related to learning can even aid in the storage and retrieval of memories. Good stress (eustress) invigorates us. It causes us to feel modestly challenged but not overwhelmed. We even feel stronger, convinced that we can rise to the occasion. Cal State Professor of Secondary Education Judy Lombardi advises, "Teaching at a slightly elevated level that is challenging but not impossible in a warm and inviting atmosphere encourages students to thrive."[2] Thus, every teaching environment needs to provide a balance of challenge and empowerment.

---

[1] Eric Jensen, *Brain-Based Learning: The New Paradigm of Teaching* (Thousand Oaks, CA: Corwin Press, 2008), 43-44.

[2] Judy Lombardi, "Beyond Learning Styles: Brain-Based Research and English-Learners," *Clearing House: A Journal of Educational Strategies, Issues, and Ideas* 81, no. 5 (May/June 2008), 222.

An additional bit of good news: Because survival can depend on knowing what to expect, we are wired to resist change and avoid conflict. Whenever a situation or question develops that challenges our beliefs, our sense of well-being is threatened. We may even go to great lengths to rationalize away compelling evidence to the contrary. Thankfully there is another side to survival. In order to survive, we have to take risks, thus, we are equally hardwired to be attracted to the new, the novel. "We survive because we are risk takers, but our goal is to stay safe by not changing an iota unless we absolutely have to. Talk about conflict!"[3] Our mind is in a constant battle, trapped choosing between stability and change, between fear and desire.

Defusing Threats to Worship

I cut my religious teeth in the evangelical tradition where "Amen" were spontaneous, frequent, and required. Hymns were fast, loose, loud, and in English. Prayer was extemporaneous. Once each month, we observed *The Lord's Supper* using grape juice and saltine crackers. And candles? They were strictly for birthday cakes.

Then one day in high school I attended mass at a local Catholic church with a friend. It had never entered my mind that I could feel uncomfortable in church––until I entered an entirely different universe of Latin, brocades, silence, written prayer, wine, candles, and chants. Through the entire service, I was two steps behind and one step to the right of everyone else, entirely unsure of what was going on, why it was going on, and what my part was in the whole drama. I chose to follow the lead of my friend. That worked quite well until I trailed behind her to the altar rail to receive the *Holy Eucharist*. There, I was asked if I was Catholic. When I answered truthfully, I was informed that I would not be allowed to participate. I wanted to slink out the back door and never return.

---

[3] Cron, Lisa, *Wired for Story: The Writer's Guide to Using Brain-Science to Hook Readers from the Very First Sentence* (New York: Ten Speed Press, 2012), 126.

Neutralizing Threats to Guests

If you have ever been a guest at a church whose worship style and rituals are considerably different from what you are used to experiencing, you know how unsure you can feel. When you feel unsure, you feel vulnerable and hesitant to move forward. Apprehensions surface as you unconsciously debate whether to proceed confidently or back away. Even though the choices you face may appear minor to some, your brain reacts as if they are important. Pointing out how insecurity affects meaning making, social psychologist and psychoanalyst Eric Fromme writes, "The quest for certainty blocks the search for meaning."[4]

Imagine the threat level experienced by a first-time guest in your church, or take it to a totally different level of threat and try to envision what is going on in the mind and body of a person who is attending a church for the first time in their life. No matter how outgoing they may appear on the surface, inside they are churning.

In one study, veterinarians used video cameras to monitor sick and injured dogs staying overnight in their facilities. They discovered that when no human was around, the dogs would lay in their enclosures listless, whimpering, vocalizing the equivalent of doggie groans, with ears limp and laid back. They exhibited every symptom of feeling miserable. Whenever a human entered the room, those same dogs often jumped to attention, wagged their tails, returned their ears to an upright position, barked playfully, and sometimes even growled as if showing dominant behavior. As soon as the human left the room, the dogs returned to their earlier behavior, once again allowing themselves to visibly suffer.

It is believed that their drastically changed behavior in the presence of a human was not because the dogs were glad to see someone. Instead, it was their way of demonstrating that they were strong enough to protect themselves if need be. They did not want to appear sick or weak before a possible opponent, so for a few moments they rallied enough to fake strength.

---

[4] Eric Fromme, *Man for Himself: An Inquiry Into The Psychology Of Ethics* (New York: Henry Holt & Co., 1947), 45.

Those first-time guests coming through your doors may very well be exhibiting the same type of behavior. They are there for a reason, and often that reason has to do with a spiritual crisis of some sort or a move to a different, unknown neighborhood. In both cases, they are already experiencing an enormous amount of stress. For them to walk into the doors of a strange church where they will experience even more uncertainty takes a great deal of courage on their part, but like those injured dogs, they will usually try to look strong and confident. It is our job to create an atmosphere of hospitality for guests by crafting an environment that removes as many threats as possible. The more threat we can eliminate in advance of their arrival, the more the guest will be able to tune in to the heart of worship.

The first line of defense should begin long before they ever enter the building. Exceptionally good directional signs in the parking lot and inside the building relieve some anxiety for those entering uncharted waters. Even more anxiety is put to rest by greeters who are trained to act as good hosts. Greeters who will walk with guests to classrooms, childcare, or the sanctuary, who will point out restrooms, who will start actual conversations with newcomers, and who will introduce them to others are worth their weight in gold.

An additional line of defense utilizes printed material. We seldom think about how often we use insider language during a service, especially during announcements and in bulletins, but to an outsider, our words might as well be Greek. Imagine that, as the worship service begins, a first-time guest hears the following announcements: *All parents should make reservations by Monday if their children plan to attend Wonderful Wednesdays. Sisters in Christ will be meeting at Clarice's home Friday at 10 am—and they should remember to bring an item for the basket they are making. Finally, parents of acolytes will be meeting briefly after worship in Parker Memorial Hall.* The guest sits there wondering, "What the heck is Wonderful Wednesday? What exactly is Sisters in Christ, and why are they making baskets? Who is Clarice? Where does she live? What is an acolyte, and where is Parker Memorial Hall?"

One of the easiest ways to alleviate this type of threat is to provide guests with a brief glossary of important terms as soon as they arrive.

Call it what you will—*The Anglican Appendix, Our Wesleyan Wordlist, Second Baptist Supplement, Valdosta Vocabulary*—have fun with it. Include all commonly used names of groups at your church with a brief explanation of why each group exists, who is invited, exactly where it meets, and if there is a childcare available. Also include a contact name and number for those wanting to learn a little more about any group before committing.

A map of the facilities should also be included. With map firmly in hand, your guests can familiarize themselves with your building without risking getting lost in a maze of hallways that all look eerily alike. Keep in mind that in most churches, locations of classrooms change on regular occasions. Accordingly, update the map with each change. Prominently numbered or named rooms will make navigating through unknown hallways even easier.

Include brief explanations of words that are specifically churchy. Does your church call your leader the *vicar*, the *priest*, the *pastor*, the *preacher*, the *rector*, the *parson*, the *reverend*, or the *minister*? Your guests need to know. Depending on the faith tradition, the words included in the glossary will vary greatly. One church may need to include *acolyte, chancel, paraments*, and *Gloria Patri,* while another church may use a totally different group of vocabulary words—*prophetic art, banners, prophesying*, and *anointing*. Always, always, always include explanations of the sacraments. I grew up in a tradition where we celebrated the Lord's Supper. I had no idea that Eucharist and Holy Communion were simply other names for the same act of worship. Neither did Ronald Reagan.

The story is told that while he was running for political office in California, Reagan was making the rounds at different churches. One Sunday, he and Nancy attended a church that celebrated Eucharist every week. The priest conducting the service, in an attempt to honor the soon-to-be governor of the state, announced that Ronald Reagan and his lovely wife Nancy were their guests that morning. He then invited them to be the first to receive the elements of the Eucharist by way of intinction. Reagan had no idea what he was talking about and was verging on total panic when Nancy whispered, "Just do what I do."

Nancy slipped out of the pew first. Her grateful husband gladly followed her to the front. Nancy took a wafer between her fingers and was about to dip it into the cup when it unexpectedly disintegrated between her fingers. A dozen pieces of wafer fell unceremoniously into the chalice. She looked up at the priest in total embarrassment and softly said, "I'm sorry, Father." As she turned to return to her seat, her husband, following her example as he had been told to do, confidently took a wafer, crushed it, and released it into the cup. Knowing that he had done the right thing in the right way, Reagan looked up with a smile on his face and said with pride, "I'm sorry, Father."

A few words of explanation in advance can prevent untold confusion and embarrassment for your guests.

Neutralizing Threats to All the Usual Suspects

Guests are not the only ones who can sense threat during worship. Without ever realizing what's going on or recognizing it for what it is, our congregation members may also be perceiving physical and emotional threats. It is therefore critical to discover and neutralize any real or imagined threats before worship ever begins. If we don't, the minds of your congregants may well be sidetracked from experiencing God's presence. We must constantly be asking, "What is happening in here that may make learning more difficult or unpleasant for this group?"

Do you remember the uncomfortably bright worship center described at the beginning of this chapter? The intense sunlight was experienced as a threat by the worshippers because it caused some to develop headaches and others to be uncomfortable. Installing light-blocking shutters that could be closed when needed neutralized that particular threat. The room was less striking in appearance, but it was also more conducive to worship.

A more common threat has to do with the temperature of the sanctuary. If people are frequently complaining that you could hang meat in the room or that the altar candles are melting even when they are not lit, you have a problem. Even though they know realistically that they will not freeze to death or suffer from heat stroke during worship, their brain is not responding to realism. It is mechanically reacting to a perceived threat.

On multiple occasions, I have heard pastors explain that they keep the sanctuary cooler than the rest of the building because they 'work up a sweat' preaching. That may or may not be because they are metaphorically 'on fire.' Because heat naturally rises, elevated stages are somewhat warmer than the lower areas of the room. Choir members can attest to the fact that it truly is hotter in the choir loft than on the main floor. Add to that situation the robes that choir members and ministers often wear over their clothing, and it is natural for them to become uncomfortably overheated.

Unfortunately, what is most comfortable for those leading worship may be very uncomfortable for those trying to worship. Endeavoring to worship in a room that is either unpleasantly cool or warm is difficult. Uncomfortable temperatures are an indisputable barrier to learning or worshipping, so a cold sanctuary may be the forerunner to a church that is cold in other ways. Consulting a professional heating and cooling expert is an essential first step in addressing this problem, but the honest reality may be that those leading worship need be the ones who change. Perhaps, in spite of tradition, they need to forgo the robes. Perhaps, they need to invest in a good deodorant and choose to be somewhat uncomfortable in order to give the congregation what they need. Otherwise, worship will suffer.

A particularly divisive problem for some churches has to do with sound levels. As a child of the '60s, I attended many loud (with a capital L) concerts. One in Tuscaloosa had the entire town vibrating to the insistent, pounding rhythm of Iron Butterfly. It was joked that their performance of *In-A-Gada-Da-Vida* that night caused tremors that were picked up by seismographs. Admittedly, the volume hurt my ears and gave me a pounding headache before it was over, but I would have never admitted it that night. I was young, foolish, under the influence, and wanted to fit in.

At that same concert, even though I had never learned to appreciate smoking, the auditorium was so thick with smoke of one kind or another that we could barely see each other. No one thought anything about it then, but just as we now know how damaging to the lungs even second-hand smoke is, we also know how dangerous loud music can be.

Our inner ears contain tiny hair cells that function as nerve endings. They carry electrical signals to the brain that are then recognized as sound. Research has proven that those hair cells are seriously damaged by loud sounds, especially prolonged loud sounds. Repeated exposure to thunderous, booming music is literally deafening. It causes hearing loss—sometimes severe hearing loss. Although I am still a fan of exuberant, enthusiastic music, I concede to the fact that I will be able to appreciate it more fully if I can still hear it five years from now. For that reason, sound levels in the church should be monitored and kept below 85 decibels to prevent irreversible injury to worshippers.

Admittedly, this stance may cause a serious conflict with those who are convinced that the louder the music is, the better the worship is. We all have personal preferences that can come across as convictions from God. I personally think it is heretical to stop in the middle of a worship service to make announcements. Others disagree. It's impossible for humans not to have preferences—and our preferences will strongly shape how we approach worship.

But *preferences are not spiritual values.* Please hear this: *Preferences are not spiritual values.* Sound level is a preference, a physical attribute that has the potential to do great good or to do serious harm. The penchant to enjoy a particular style of music is strongly influenced by our culture, not our faith. Before drawing a line in the sand over an issue that has nothing whatsoever to do with following Jesus, remember that.

Make sure all those who help lead worship are aware of the facts and understand what the risks are. Remember that they are not your opponents. They may in fact be deeply committed, faithful, godly people who invest time daily praying about how to use their talents to lead people to the throne of God. Take time to pray regularly with them about this and other issues. Encourage them to try leading music that falls within the recommended guidelines for a few weeks. They may be surprised at the number of compliments they receive from grateful worshippers. Nevertheless, expect some to complain. When they do, remind yourself and your colleagues that no matter what you do or how you do it, somebody will always complain. That is a given.

Another huge threat is perceived whenever we are asked to do something that is impossible to do. I was once ordered by a senior pastor to schedule and plan two very large events for the church—both occurring on the same day, at the same time, using the same sanctuary. I tried to explain to my boss that it was a physical impossibility, that to do so I would have to know how to alter the space-time continuum. His response was a growled, "I don't want to hear excuses. Make it happen." To say that at that moment I was experiencing a real sense of threat—and frustration and anger and weariness—would be an understatement.

We all feel threatened when asked to do the impossible. We've all been in situations when we were asked to do a task but were not given what we needed to complete it, whether what we needed was information, material resources, or financial resources. For this reason, whenever a supplemental activity is included in worship, it is critical to make sure all materials are in place and in working order well before the service begins. (You'll learn more about supplemental activities in the next chapter.) If, for example, you are going to ask the participant to pray for homebound members, don't forget to provide their names and circumstances (when appropriate). If you are going to invite congregants to draw a prayer, make sure the drawing materials are immediately available. If a computer will be included as part of an activity, make sure it is connected and fully working long before the service begins so it can be used by the first person who arrives. Omitting even one needed resources for an activity is self-defeating behavior for those who desire to design effective worship.

Another threat comes when we are asked to deal with too much new information at once. Remember those high school physics classes that left your head spinning? Even though our mind works as a parallel processor, there is only so much new input it can deal with at one time. When learning new information, the brain is already somewhat stressed. When asked to learn too much information, it goes into cognitive overload. Imagine the difference between being asked to memorize a significant verse in a day as opposed to being asked to memorize an entire chapter in a day. You know you can do the first. You can't imagine doing the second.

Learning is always hindered when we try to pack too much information into an already busy brain—especially unnecessary material. Think of it this way: If you are packing for a trip, you may reach a point when your suitcase simply cannot contain all the paraphernalia you are trying to stuff into it. At that point, you must begin a triage process of deciding what to carry and what to leave behind.

Before teaching ever begins, the best teachers eliminate everything except what directly points to the material to be learned, knowing that doing so reduces the stress level of the learner and frees up additional memory for the more important issues. They present material in small, bite-sized, manageable blocks, knowing it will have a cumulative effect over time.

When writing a sermon, it is imperative to leave out all extraneous material. If something can be eliminated and the point still made, jettison it. No matter how tempting, never give in to the temptation to chase rabbits, to run down unrelated trails, or to share your interesting vacation experiences with a captive audience. Because unrelated material only hinders pattern formation, it should be scrupulously avoided.

If you are preaching about Daniel, the history of Persia may be fascinating to you, but no one really wants you to demonstrate that you can name the last five kings of Persia. If you are a huge football fan, good for you—but don't waste the precious memory capacity of your listeners with jokes about your opponents. Jokes can capture attention and aid learning, but they are counterproductive unless they relate directly to the point you are making. One of the most loving things you can do for your flock is to provide precise, well-thought-out teaching and explanation with no superfluous details.

One last bit of important information: Keep in mind that if you are preaching to an audience already familiar with a subject, less oral instruction is actually needed. On the other hand, if you are preaching to learners who have little or no previous knowledge of the subject matter, more direct oral instruction, guidance, and explanation will be needed and appreciated.

Now we are about to investigate the one threat that outweighs all others. Don't be surprised if you recognize yourself somewhere in the next chapter.

Chapter 6

REMEMBER TO RELEASE CONTROL

She was back at home after completing her first year of college, and I was thrilled. As her mother, I was excited about the chance to spend a little uninterrupted time with her. As a nineteen-year-old, she was more interested in getting out of the house and catching up with old friends.

Before she left to do so, she stated that she needed to put a load of laundry in the washer. Minutes later, as she walked through the kitchen with her laundry basket, I informed her that I had just purchased a container of what was supposedly a miracle laundry brightener. "You're welcome to give it a try if you want."

Her shrill-voiced reaction resembled that of a honey badger defending her young. "*Mother!* I have been washing my own clothes for over a year now *without* your help! I *know* what I'm doing. I *don't* need your advice. Would you just *stop* trying to tell me how to live my life?"

Three days later, she called home from a newer restaurant saying she had heard me mention eating there before. "What should I order for lunch?" was her question. Without mentioning her name, my advice sounded somewhat like this: "*Daughter!* You have been ordering your own food for over a year now *without* my help! You *know* what you're doing. You *don't* need my advice. I've got to *stop* trying to tell you how to live your life!"

I can laugh because I remember being of the exact same mind when I was her age. It was November. Only weeks before, I had registered to vote for the first time in a Presidential election. On the Sunday before the Tuesday election, I dropped by my parents' home. Before leaving, my father handed me the mock ballot from that morning's newspaper on which he had marked his voting preferences for every race, advising "Here's who you need to vote for Tuesday." My reaction to his offer of 'help' was very similar to my daughter's reaction. I was highly offended that he thought he could dictate my choices, so I let him know it—shall I say—with intensity.

Give Choice a Chance

No one, absolutely no, one likes to feel controlled. You were born fighting any attempt to be dominated by another person. If you don't believe it, just try telling a two-year-old that they cannot do something. Even if they have never considered trying to do it in the first place, they seem to take your directive as a dare, not a demand. Feeling controlled in any way, physically or mentally, is a highly intimidating form of threat at any age.

When someone else determines what you must learn and how you must learn it, your brain rebels at every opportunity. Leaders of *VitalSmarts* (innovators in corporate training and organizational performance) insist that offering choices to adults is the "gateway to all other methods of influencing personal motivation. . . . You can never hope to engage people's commitment if they don't have permission to say no. . . . It almost doesn't matter how small the encroachment on our agency; we've been known to go to war over it."[1]

If you are allowed to make even small choices about what and how you learn, you feel more valued and less threatened. Although the teacher must necessarily fix the parameters within which the learner will work, providing choices is the foundation for deeper learning. Adult-education consultants Harold Stolovich and Erica Keeps state, "The principle of autonomy in adult learning centers on the fact that adults actively engage in their day-to-day decision making. So should

---

[1] Joseph Grenny et al., *Influencer: The New Science of Leading Change*, 2d ed. (New York: McGraw-Hill, 2013), 84.

they in their learning. The more they contribute, the more ownership they create for themselves."[2]

Research demonstrates that it is not necessary to give learners a choice in everything; even occasional choices are tremendously beneficial. The best learning environments provide multiple activities from which learners can choose simply because of individual preference. However if the activities are to be beneficial (and this is crucial), each activity must relate directly to the subject matter to be learned.

Dial it Down

Less obvious, but just as threatening is a leader who has a domineering or overwhelming personality. Confidence is a good thing. Confidence that borders on arrogance or intimidation is not. Stories are widespread of pastors who function more like dictators than shepherds. I once worked with one who enjoyed flaunting his position as senior pastor, incessantly reminding the congregation and staff that he was in charge. He used the *pastoral authority* card to address every issue, no matter how trivial—from what color paint was used in a classroom to what plants were installed in the flowerbeds.

The truth is, the more often one has to remind others that they have authority, the less genuine authority they actually have. As a matter of fact, a leader who keep reminding everyone that he or she is in charge is engaging in self-destructive behavior, behavior indicative of a power trip that causes the brains of their listeners to scream, "Danger! Watch out! That person wants to control you!"

They may be totally mistaken, but the listeners' intuitions and suspicions have a powerful influence on how they react to both the person speaking and the message he or she brings. As a rule of thumb, self-promotion is a one-way street that inevitably leads to mistrust, and mistrust is a very real threat that naturally culminates in fight or flight—either of which can quickly become a life-or-death issue in a struggling church.

---

[2] Harold D. Stolovitch and Erica J. Keeps, *Telling Ain't Training* (Alexandria, VA: American Society for Training & Development, 2011), 68.

You can prevent that kind of pain for everyone involved by embodying the role of a servant without ever mentioning that you are the designated leader. Your people already know that. Besides, Jesus never called you to lead; he called you to follow him. You are but one follower among many, all of whom follow best when they call no attention to their own service. Instead of being your own biggest fan, you should consistently direct all attention and any credit for success to Jesus while expressing gratitude to all the others who are walking in his footsteps without elevating themselves. If you really want to see your church grow stronger in faith and deeper in her commitment to follow Jesus, make a point of acknowledging other individuals in public for their acts of service and their good ideas. Brag about them behind their backs and to their faces. Forget about blowing your own horn and let others know that they are appreciated and loved. The more you decrease your own self-promotion, the more Christ increases, and the more people will be willing to listen attentively to what God may have to say through you.

Speaking of which, speaking from the pulpit is always speaking from a position of power. Abuses of power can surface in a multitude of ways. For example, one of my preaching professors joked that he had seen notes from a sermon with the following written in the margin: *Weak point. Talk louder. Pound pulpit.* Be aware that when forceful language is used too often from the pulpit, the listeners can interpret it as an attempt to control them by suppressing their opinions or even shaming them into 'acceptable behavior.' The old English word for *threat* means *pressure*. When we apply pressure by our manner of speaking, it is seldom as subtle as we think. Most of our congregants already understand the power dynamics that are at play in a church. They prefer that we be open and honest about our motives. Anything else is manipulation.

You will make considerably more impact on people by exuding a quiet enthusiasm, by receiving criticism without becoming defensive, and by modeling vulnerability, transparency, risk taking, and even doubt. In doing so, you are empowering your listeners to take chances themselves, to be real, to struggle with their own doubt in a healthy way, to consider troubling alternatives to their beliefs that they might otherwise try to avoid, to challenge authority, and to take control of their own spiritual development. This leads directly to the next point.

Defusing the Control Issue

As mentioned earlier, all people of all ages, races, ethnic groups, and economic levels categorically despise being controlled. They don't enjoy it at home, at work, or in church. Anytime they feel as if they are under someone else's power, their threat response kicks in. Whenever a person feels that they have no choice but to do what they are told, they resent it. If the only choices are to comply or defy, they are in what is ultimately a lose-lose situation. If, however, you can somehow enable your congregants to make choices on regular occasions, even small choices, you are putting them in the metaphorical driver's seat, thus decreasing the threat level dramatically. When allowed to make choices for themselves, they feel less threatened, more valued, and will learn more.

Although the one doing the teaching will necessarily give the parameters within which the learning will occur, providing choices within those parameters greatly increases enthusiasm to learn and participate. Considering that the members of your congregation actively engage in making significant decisions every day of their life—at home, at work, at school, and at play—it is only natural that they will be comfortable doing the same in worship, yet the worship service is one of the few places where they have little to no say-so in what they are going to do or how they are going to do it.

Research demonstrates that the more autonomy a person has in learning anything, the more likely they are to take ownership of what is learned, to contribute to the group experience, and to act on the information they are taking in. Distinguished University Professor Stephen Brookfield, of The University of St. Thomas in Minneapolis-St. Paul, notes, "The point of learning is thought to be the development in learners of a sense of agency—a belief that they can accomplish something they previously had considered unattainable or that they had never even imagined."[3]

Is this not the very essence of transformation? As Christ-followers take ownership of their own discipleship, they are being transformed into the image of Jesus. As this happens, they contribute more of their life to the Church by sharing their own experiences with other followers and by acting on what they are learning. They develop an understanding of how Jesus lives in and works through them as he empowers them for active engagement with a broken world. As Jesus is incarnated in them, he heals them, and through them, he heals others, doing more than the believer could ever ask for or imagine.

Thankfully, it is not necessary to give learners a choice in everything they do, but when given regular choices about how to approach a subject, confidence soars. Participation and enthusiasm to act on what is learned increase exponentially. In short, the best learning environments provide multiple activities from which learners can choose simply because of their individual preferences. Always keep in mind that the components of the activities must be coherent, meaningful, and directly related to the lesson being taught if they are to be beneficial. When they are, the resulting combination of variety, choice, and the natural motivation to learn works magic, turning any teaching time into an experience instead of a chore.

What Would the Choices Look Like?

Choices can come in the form of supplemental activities available before, during, or after the worship service. Those activities should include both structured activities for the left-brain and more artistic, creative activities for the right, but all learners can benefit from either type of activity. Even though there is evidence that the brain has a preferred learning style, and that there is a biological difference between right-brain activity and left-brain activity, "The importance of addressing a more favored sense is small compared with structure, response,

---

[3] Stephen D. Brookfield, *Powerful Techniques for Teaching Adults* (San Francisco, CA: Jossey-Bass, 2013), 10.

feedback, and use of multisensory stimulation."[4] The hemispheres of the brain are always interacting, no matter what type of information is introduced, so they derive meaning from each other. That said, the right brain has been neglected for so long that the mere inclusion of activities that play on its strength will be revolutionary for some.

Supplemental activities can include visual, auditory, tactile, olfactory, gustatory, and kinesthetic components.[5] A variety of activities will allow learners to make choices for themselves and to learn from their strengths. The act of making those choices will in fact prepare them to be less resistant and more receptive to the oral teaching of the sermon.

One of the most effective ways to facilitate choices during worship is by using small tables, or stations, prepared beforehand and placed to the rear and the sides of the worship center. Each station needs to be interactive. An effective station is more than just an attractive visual display. It must always includes some way that the worshipper can interact with it—completing an activity, adding to it, or giving meaning to it in their own way.

Each station must relate directly to the theme of worship for the day if it is to be beneficial. If, for instance, you are preaching about prayer, an activity on stewardship will do nothing to enhance the learning experience. However, if you set up several participatory prayer stations with appropriate prompts, people will experience prayer as a reality rather than a theoretical possibility. Each station should offer a different activity. In this case, they could include:

- A display listing homebound members and members in nursing homes with specific suggestions for their prayer needs. Also include pens, index cards, and a small box so that anyone interested in adopting a person for whom they prayed can leave their name and contact information in the box. (Be sure to follow-up with anyone who volunteers within forty-eight hours.)

---

[4] Harold D. Stolovich and Erica Keeps, Beyond Telling Ain't Training Fieldbook (Alexandria, VA: American Society for Training and Development), 114.

[5] These will be discussed in more depth in chapter 7.

- A table that includes a large bowl of water, several hand towels, a poster with Psalm 51:10 ("Create in me a new heart, O God"), and another poster with instructions inviting participants to pray about any area in which their heart needs to be cleansed, and then afterwards symbolically wash and dry their hands.
- A table with laptops opened to your church's website, index cards, pencils, push pins, and a corkboard. Posted instructions would invite participants to navigate through the different ministries, choose one, write a short prayer for it, and post it on the corkboard.
- A table with white cardstock, colored markers, colored pencils, pushpins, a large corkboard, and instructions inviting participants to 'draw' a prayer for an unnamed individual or group. Afterwards, they should post it anonymously on the corkboard.

Some will immediately welcome such new elements in the worship service. Others will view the very invitation to participate in a hands-on activity as a threat. If you are in an older church, it would be extremely wise to begin with only one or two stations located in the rear of the sanctuary or in the entryway of the church. At first, offer simple activities that will not require too much from those who participate. After a few months, add an additional station. Continue to add stations as time passes. If my experience holds true, after a few months, even the most hesitant members will join in as they discover that everyone benefits when invited to energetically use their minds and take control of their own discipleship.

Many evangelical churches already include a time to respond to the sermon, often called the invitation. Traditionally, it is a time for people to go to the front of the sanctuary to talk to the pastor or kneel and pray at the altar rail. Consider offering the congregation multiple ways to respond during this time. For example, while quiet music plays, invite those present to use the time to respond to what they have experienced in worship in whatever way they are comfortable. Let them know that they can respond

- By going into an adjoining room to pray with a group of people
- By remaining seated exactly where they are to pray
- By speaking with one of several ministers stationed around the room
- By coming to a station to receive communion
- By writing a prayer or prayer poem on a graffiti wall at the rear of the sanctuary
- By signing up for a ministry opportunity related to the sermon at another station
- By leaving questions at a station that will help guide the direction of future services
- By dropping a small pebble into a large kiddie pool filled with water to observe the ripple effects, symbolizing how a prayer said here can make an impact far away

While working in a church that conducted that kind of invitation, I watched the membership learn that church was a safe place to take risks—to ask off-the-wall questions and give original answers no one had programmed them to give. Young adults who had been sporadic, passive attenders began to sign up for ministry opportunities, serving both inside and outside the church building. Their attendance at services became more regular. They grew more comfortable praying with and for others. Several who had never considered inviting someone to church began to bring friends. Others got involved in small groups before and after the service. With the participants using both their brains and their bodies to worship, we saw the resulting transformation with our own eyes.

Chapter 7

MULTISENSORY MEMORIES

In Washington D.C., along with a multitude of others, I slowly wound my way through the meandering paths and the display rooms of The Holocaust Museum. At a snail's pace, we filed past captioned photos of victims and victimizers. We paused inside an actual cattle car that had been used to transport doomed human cargo to Dachau. We viewed an original copy of the infamous *The Protocols of the Elders of Zion*, touched the iron doors to a crematorium, and watched the filmed testimonies of rare survivors. The surreal experience left me mercifully numb.

The numbness evaporated in an instant when I entered a long corridor filled with nothing but old shoes piled upon more old shoes—graceful feminine shoes, sturdy work shoes, children's button-top shoes, gentleman's shoes, tiny toddler shoes, dusty, scuffed, well-worn shoes—shoes that had been confiscated from those entering the gas chambers. Confronted by these aging artifacts that represented a multitude of unrealized dreams that literally went up in smoke, I was overwhelmed with emotion.

Surprisingly, the emotion was not caused by the way the shoes looked. It was caused by the way they smelled. They smelled of old leather. They also smelled of feet. The smell of their ill-fated owners lingered some sixty years after the fact, testifying to the reality of their lives and reeking with the obscenity of their deaths. This powerfully invasive and unexpected olfactory sensation tapped into something deep within me. I began to sob.

Until the 1980s, odor was considered a mortal enemy of museums. Smells of any kind, treated as pollution brought in by the unclean masses, were therefore strictly forbidden. According to art historian Jim Drobnick (Ontario College of Art and Design), since the late eighteenth century, museums and other public spaces have waged an unrelenting deodorizing campaign. They spent decades intentionally and unashamedly attempting to erase unpleasant human odors because they staunchly associated unpleasant smells with the lower classes—the homeless, ethnic groups, minimum wage workers, and immigrants. "The rationale of hygiene as a tool for social engineering and/or exclusion is one that continues to this day; advocates for the homeless must continue to go to court to protect access to libraries and other public places."[1]

In a surprising about-face, today's museums embrace smell as an important dimension of the museum experience. Subtle odors from exhibits mix with more refined fragrances from gift shops and mouth-watering aromas from in-house restaurants. Museums are intentionally infusing their exhibits with appropriate smells, ranging from the crisp smell of fresh-cut grass in an 'American Lawn' exhibit to the smell of urine and garbage in an 'Inner City Life' exhibit at the Smithsonian.[2]

What has caused the dramatic shift from the sterilized museum of 1960 to the urine-scented displays of today? Why are similar sensory modifications taking place in shopping malls, amusement parks, and universities? Along that same line of thought, how should the Church respond to this development?

Presently, the Church is perceived as having an aversion to the very senses designed by God. Scripture, however, appeals to the senses at every turn. Leonard Sweet observes, "Biblical Israel was a sensory culture with a religious fluency in all five senses."[3] Exodus describes the visual, olfactory, and audible intricacies of God's own plan for the Tabernacle. The Song of Solomon uses the imagery of intimacy and erotic desire. Isaiah paints an unsettling and graphic picture of the

---

[1] David Howes, ed., *Empire of the Senses: The Sensual Cultural Reader* (New York: Berg Publishers, 2005), 267.

[2] Ibid., 270.

[3] Leonard Sweet, *Nudge: Awakening Each Other to the God Who's Already There* (Colorado Springs: David C. Cook, 2010), 270.

Suffering Servant experiencing raw corporeal pain. Paul celebrates the Incarnation in which God, equipped with human sensory capabilities, engaged in the ordinary acts of eating, touching, tasting, smelling, seeing, feeling pain, and feeling pleasure. John's invitation to "Come and see" was grounded in the fact that he personally saw, heard, and touched Jesus. Scripture is swimming in an ocean of sensory images; yet, today the word *sensual* is seldom even whispered in churches.

Sensual Christianity

The church has been suspicious of the senses throughout her history. Fourth-century church father Augustine wrote that the devil "places himself in figures, he adapts himself to colors, he attaches himself to sounds, he lurks in angry and wrongful conversation, he abides in smells, he impregnates with flavors, and fills with certain exhalations all the channels of the understanding." Even so, Augustine grudgingly conceded that "our sense of perception, when it is grounded in faith, allows us to see the world as signs of a deeper reality."[4] Fortunately, because the church valued both trains of his thought, "traditional Christian anthropology has always clearly insisted that sense knowledge and spiritual knowledge constitute a unity, and that all spiritual knowledge, however sublime it may be, is initiated and filled with content by sense experience."[5]

Fourteenth-century poet Dante embraced the sensual. Convinced that the world "shines with borrowed beauty," he insisted that it is through such beauty that God reveals himself to humanity. Dante observed beauty not only in the material creation; he also witnessed it in the sensuality of the liturgy, of song, and of dance. Confident in the belief that humans receive revelation through their senses, he saw the purpose of that revelation (and the purpose of life) to be a gradual "purgation of one's besetting sins and a progressive attachment

---

[4] William A. Dyrness, *Poetic Theology* (Grand Rapids, MI: William Eerdmans Publishing Company, 2011), 149.

[5] Ibid., 166.

to those things in which God can be seen and loved."⁶ *The Divine Comedy* exhibits how Dante used lush sensory imagery toward the goal of inspiring love of God. Dante described God as being at work revealing himself to humanity, dropping hints about who He is throughout his creation because he is a God who desires to be known. The 'knowing' that Dante's writing promoted was not predominately intellectual knowledge. It was personal, intimate knowledge of a God who was already present, who was actively creating beauty to capture humanity's attention, and who was perpetually conveying his self-revelation through the human senses.

Some two hundred and fifty years later, John Bunyan painted a more austere picture of God's relationship with his creation. In *Pilgrim's Progress*, Bunyan described a world filled with temptation and trial, a world in which material goods and sensory pleasures are treacherous snares to be avoided. Bunyan viewed the senses as obstacles to more rational knowledge. He believed that one best comes to know God intellectually, guided by a written text that must be carefully read and interpreted. The hero of his story became the unshakable paradigm for a new version of Christianity, one in which head knowledge replaced an earlier emphasis on sensory experience.

With Bunyan, an epistemological revolution had begun. Describing this development, William Dyrness, Professor of Theology and Culture at Fuller Theological Seminary, contends that the church exchanged involvement of the lower body in worship—prostrating self, kneeling, dancing—for involvement of the upper body, especially the head. "With their frequent sermons and regular catechism, Reformers insisted that understanding should replace sensual bodily experience of objects and practices. . . . Believers in Geneva were to close their eyes and listen: they were to think and not adore."⁷

Bunyan's writing, coupled with the Renaissance's corresponding emphasis on empiricism and scientific objectivity, resulted in an age characterized by an increasing distrust of sensory information. The Protestant church, which previously had lavishly used visual images (icons, statues, and stained glass), fragrances (incense), sounds (bells,

---

⁶ Dyrness, *Poetic Theology*, 156.

⁷ Dyrness, *Poetic Theology*, 139.

choirs, chants, and instruments), and tactile elements (rich fabrics, anointing oils, and wood or stone carvings), abandoned them for an intellectualized version of faith. In this era of disembodied 'knowing,' dualism reigned as undisputed king. "Since Reformers believed that truth had to be appropriated internally through the hearing of the word, what was grasped inwardly by the working of the mind came to have more authority than what was experienced through the bodily life in the world, and accordingly, intellectual life came to be valued above the affective life."[8]

Tasting Sound and Hearing Sight

In the past, we have thought of the senses as operating individually, each sending information directly to a specialized area of the brain designed to deal with input from that specific sense organ. For example, we have long known that one area of the brain (the primary auditory cortex) is responsible for processing sound, but we assumed sound was all it processed. Recent research shows that the same area also plays a role in processing visual and tactile stimuli. In other words, our eyes and fingers are connected to our ears. Our fingers are linked to our tongue. Our ears are networked with our nose. Not only are our brain and body fused, our senses and our brain are proving to be mingled.

Because the brain is a parallel processor, every sense is processed through multiple pathways. This ability, called *dual coding*, allows the same sensory information to enter the system through multiple channels. If one channel is 'blocked,' another channel will circumvent it—thus the proverbial blind woman with a heightened sense of sound and smell or the deaf man who feels music.

Although Western civilization remains mired in gray matter, today's scholars are enthusiastically revisiting the concept of knowledge that results from direct sensory experience. Research in neuroscience is proving that our responses, thoughts, actions, and memories are all informed as our body interrogates the world, collects physical stimuli, and fuses it with historical and cultural details. In other words, meaning

---

[8] Dyrness, *Poetic Theology,* 167

arises as our mind conducts a complex juggling act with immediate sensory input, past experience, and enculturated norms.

In many ways, the brain does not even care which sense organ provides it with information. For instance, at times you 'see' what you hear. It is a common experience to hear someone drop something in the next room and know immediately what was dropped simply from the sound it makes.

Even in the most ordinary circumstances, our senses inform each other. In one study, subjects were blindfolded and guided into totally darkened rooms that they had never seen before. Amazingly, they could tell quite a few things about the room using their ears alone. They could recognize from a hollow sound if they were led into a staircase or from an echo that the space they entered was very large. They could determine the gender of unseen individuals walking across the room simply by listening to their footsteps (regardless of shoe style). They could even tell if the individuals were walking upright or were walking while slumped over. When wooden rods were dropped, "listeners could determine the length of the rods with impressive accuracy simply by hearing them hit the floor."[9]

When asked to listen to a series of flat steel plates struck by a metal pendulum and identify if the plates were shaped like a square, a circle, or a triangle, they were uncannily capable of doing so. According to University of California's Professor of Psychology Lawrence Rosenblum, "It is likely that your sense of general size, shape, and material of objects is based as much on your hearing as on your vision. . . . The unconscious brain is constantly processing reflected sound. . . . Our brains use changes in reflected sound to know that something in the environment is different."[10] This process aids us in our never-ending vigilant quest to survive, allowing us to often hear danger before we ever see it.

Sound even influences how things taste. In one experiment, subjects were asked to bite ninety potato chips one time each. They were to then spit the bite out before judging its crispness. The chips were, unknown to the subjects, all Pringles from the same batch. A microphone was

---

[9] Lawrence D. Rosenblum, *See What I'm Saying: The Extraordinary Powers of Our Five Senses* (New York: W. W. Norton & Company, 2010), 40.

[10] Rosenblum, *See What I'm Saying,* 14.

positioned at the lips so the subjects could hear the amplified chewing sounds. "Sounds were modified electronically by manipulating the loudness and timbre (brightness) heard by the subjects.... In general, the louder and brighter the sound, the fresher the chips were judged to be. If the sound was quieter and duller, the chips 'tasted' stale."[11] Hence, taste is the result of what happens not only on our tongues, but also in our ears, eyes, and especially noses. Similar results have been found with all senses; none act alone.

We are all familiar with stories of people who have lost one sense such as sight and compensate for it with other senses. Surprisingly, even when all sensory channels are fully functioning, greater total information can be processed when it is presented through multiple sensory channels. Information that is received through more than one sense is more securely stored in the memory than that which is learned through the input of only one sense. Why? The information has been imprinted along more than one sensory pathway. When information is stored along multiple, distinct pathways, the brain has multiple ways it can access that information.

Think of it this way: Sensory information is not confined to a single, narrow road that runs directly from a sense organ to the brain and back again. Instead, in its never-ending journey, it can choose from the multiple lanes of an interstate highway, lanes that repeatedly intersect, connect, and crisscross to form a network of expressways that run throughout the body. A signal that is picked up through touch may actually be routed through the part of the brain that deals with hearing or taste before it's over. When we are bombarded by multiple sensory signals, our senses work in tandem to feed information to the brain. The brain then integrates those various signals to help make sense of our surroundings.

For every sense activated during a learning experience, a different sensory pathway is opened and can be re-activated in remembering the event. The more 'felt' qualities there are to any information being conveyed, the easier the information is to remember and the more likely a person is to act on said information. The more physically engaged a

---

[11] Rosenblum, *See What I'm Saying*, 107

learner is with a subject, the more likely what is learned will result in significant change in the behavior and thinking patterns of the learner.

Nevertheless, humans are visual animals. Although all sense organs route information to the brain and body, sight is the primary sense through which we receive information—eighty-five percent of the information we take in each day is visual. The retina contains forty percent of all nerve fibers connected to the brain. Almost half of our brain is devoted to the seeing process. Vision is so important that the brain prioritizes visual information over everything else.

In a stunning study by Harvard graduate Chia-Jung Tsay, participants (including several highly trained musicians) were asked to watch a video of pianists playing in a classical music competition with the sound turned off. The same subjects were later asked to listen to the same performances (in a different order), this time without seeing the video. In nearly all cases, participants were "better able to identify the winners of classical music competitions by watching silent video clips than by listening to audio recordings. . . . The effect held up even in high-level international competitions, which often feature not only top performers, but also highly trained musicians as judges."[12] In this situation, one would have expected audio information to have been much more important than visual information. It wasn't.

Teaching any kind of material through the use of only one sense fails to make the most of our God-designed ability to learn in multisensory environments. Remarkably though, recent research has unexpectedly proven that when learners are regularly introduced to multisensory experiences, subsequent unisensory processing also improves. This means that we do not have to make every element of a learning experience multi-sensory. If we include some multisensory input however, the learners' unisensory detection, discrimination, and recognition is greatly enriched.

Lecture alone limits learning to an auditory event. When visuals are added, the information is carried over an additional neural pathway. If other senses are involved in ways that directly relate to the material,

---

[12] Peter Ruell, "The Look of Music," *Harvard Gazette* (August 19, 2013), accessed August 21, 2013. http://news.harvard.edu/gazette/story/2013/08/the-look-of-music/.

even more neural pathways are activated. Mental activity accelerates further when a hands-on activity is incorporated. Optimal learning occurs when, along with hearing well-prepared content, a learner manipulates objects or symbols associated with the content, engages in role-play, experiences appropriate aromas or tastes, and sees visuals that connect to the content. The more senses involved, the stronger the memory is stored.

Communication never happens in a vacuum. It happens in a physical, concrete, culturally shaped world. We engage with objects and persons in the materiality of our bodies using our senses. Knowing this should immediately cause us "to reconsider, profoundly, the separation of categories such as mind and body, of cognition and affect."[13] Simply put, multisensory stimulation that accompanies the teaching of content can be used to strengthen the memory, to motivate passion to pursue further learning, and to spur the learner to take action on what has been learned.

Sensual Worship

Just because a minster spends days composing a sermon, and then presents it flawlessly, verbalizing every point and every single application, it does not mean that the sermon has been communicated. Talking does not necessarily result in listening. Children learn that lesson early.

By the time our oldest daughter was six years old, she and her sisters had already learned to ask their father dodgy questions while he was watching television. With his attention diverted, they would ease up to him—out of his line of site—and softly pose a question to which they knew they would typically get a 'No.' "Daddy, will you take us to Chuck E. Cheese after the news goes off?" "Daddy, can we eat ice cream and cookies for breakfast?" "Daddy, can we go outside and shoot bottle rockets at each other?" Without ever really listening, he would mumble, "Mmm-Hmmm," or "Sure." The results were often laughable.

---

[13] Ruell, "The Look of Music," 77.

Those who strive to communicate the Gospel know the same thing happens all too often in worship. Just because we may be talking, there is no guarantee anyone is listening. It does not have to stay that way. If we want to effectively communicate the most important missive ever given, we should be willing to make use of every means possible to do so. Brain research demonstrates that because humans learn most naturally as they process multiple sources of input about the same subject, the most effective way to communicate the Gospel is to connect spoken word to other modes of communication. Every mode has potential for meaning. This potential is best realized as we create complementary arrangements of multiple modes. Doing so allows new doorways for understanding to be opened.

Our sacramental rituals are already sensory-drenched, meaning-constructing activities that "place knowledge in the realm of the senses rather than just in the realm of increasing abstraction."[14] The sensory elements of communion and baptism claim our attention and awaken our mind, inviting us to 're-member,' to put the pieces of life and faith back together. This power should not be restricted to the sacraments. While preparing sermons or lessons, we need to constantly ask ourselves, "How can this be made visible or tangible?" while simultaneously asking God to enliven both our imagination and the written word.

Like nothing else, smell triggers memories and transports us through time. Every church should have a distinct, consistent smell signature. Be it incense, sandalwood, or lavender, after a time, the scent itself will begin to evoke past 'God-moments' for those present. Smell can also be used in specific teaching moments: myrrh-scented cloths strips tied around wrists when preaching the story of Lazarus' burial, perfume wafting through the sanctuary for the story of the woman who anointed Jesus, even stable smells for the nativity story. Jonah? Open a few cans of sardines and hide them around the sanctuary the night before. It may not be perfume, but it will be memorable.

Teaching should always be image-rich. Images are a universal language that can build bridges between what the learner already knows and any new information they are receiving. Vivid and emotionally

---

[14] Joddy Murray, *Non-Discursive Rhetoric: Image and Affect in Multimodal Composition* (Albany: SUNY Press, 2009), 1.

saturated images can stir up surprising reactions. Incorporating images in any teaching situation is a natural way to grab attention. In many cases, images can allow the learner to experience what is only a theoretical concept when presented exclusively in words.

Narrative sermons acquire visual impact when the large screen is utilized like a picture book. Imagine telling the creation story with images of nature on the big screen that change with each of the seven days. Sometimes symbolic representations of the story work best. If a metaphor can be found to capture the essence of the sermon—for instance a potter to represent transformation—keep different images of that metaphor on the screen, changing throughout the service. Incorporate the selected visuals on altars, in entryways, on bulletins, and at activity stations. These images allow God's Word to be seen, heard, felt, smelled, and tasted.

Wonderful images can be found online, sometimes free. At other times, you may need to pay a small fee to use them. Good sources for cheap images are *Google, StockVault, CanStockPhoto, Dreamstime,* and *iStockPhoto.* The selected images can be projected or printed. For projected images, make sure to purchase larger versions of the images. For printed images, the small ones do fine. Other sites, such as *SermonSpice, Midnight Oil Productions,* and *Worship House Media,* produce powerful but short videos related to major themes of Scripture. It may take a while to learn to navigate the sites, but it is well worth your time to supplement the service with these outstanding visuals. Minds will not wander as your congregants watch.

Touch? The congregation can be invited to hold hands during Prayers of the People (if they are comfortable doing so) in recognition of the fact that Jesus touched every person he healed. Sometimes we need to be touched by God. Sometimes we need to be touched by other people, by people who share in our journey. Prayer time is a good opportunity to give the congregation to do so. Touch can be used to emphasize parts of a sermon. Listeners can be given a heavy stone to grip during a sermon about the woman caught in adultery. They can be invited to flex, touch, and observe the miracle of their own hand when you preach on Psalm 139. They can be asked, "How much is a life worth?" while holding a check as you preach on the betrayal of Judas. If the subject for the day is prayer, everyone can be invited to take out his or her cell phone and add a contact number for a 24-hour prayer line that you recommend.

Taste? Invite them to bite into a fresh fig before preaching a sermon of hope from Jeremiah 24. Before a sermon about Samson, serve mini-biscuits drizzled with local honey to those entering the building. Along with the Passover story, offer horseradish on matzo bread to symbolize the bitterness of slavery or sprigs of parsley dipped in salty water to symbolize the tears shed. When preaching on the "Living Water," illustrate the concept by having a large clear container of stagnant water dipped from a puddle on the altar. Beside it, place a fountain filled with running water. No one has to actually taste the stagnant water to understand it will not support life.

Sound? Preach the flood story while a soundtrack of rain or animal sounds plays in the background. Ask someone to blow a shofar for a sermon on repentance (You may be able to borrow one from your local synagogue). Begin a Pentecost sermon with the sound of a mighty wind. Preaching on Samson? As you walk to the pulpit, play the theme from *Rocky*. Gideon? Have several people unexpectedly slam a terra cotta flowerpot down on the ground at the back of the room at the appropriate time during the story. The sound of a rooster crowing would be very appropriate for the betrayal of Peter.

The teacher needs to remain aware of two problems intrinsic to multisensory teaching. First, it is possible to over-stimulate the senses to the point that they become a threat to learning. A study conducted by cognitive neuroscientist Rachel Herz revealed occasions when multisensory stimulation interfered with concentration.[15] If, for example, you have ever sat near someone wearing an overpowering fragrance, you know how disconcerting it can be. It's difficult to pay attention to anything else when you can't breathe. In addition, sound that is too loud distracts rather than adds to a message. Second, education specialists Charles Fadel and Cheryl Lemke caution against redundancy. The exact same material should not be presented simultaneously in different modes. Scrolling text across the bottom of a video that already has sound only distracts the learner. It would be preferable to wait

---

[15] Rachel S. Herz, "Odor-associative Learning and Emotion: Effects on Perception and Behavior," *Oxford Journals* 30, no. 1 (2005): 250-251.

until the video is over and teach the same information using a different mode.[16] Keep in mind that, as noted earlier, there is no such thing as too many visuals, but when supplementing a sermon with other sensory input, think sequential and not simultaneous. Target only one sense at a time. Of course, it will be almost impossible to stimulate only one sense, but by intentionally focusing on one at a time, you will be less likely to provoke any form of unconscious resistance in the learner.

The possibilities of involving senses to reinforce the teaching of the sermon are limited only by your imagination. When using sensory stimulation however, use it with discretion. Anything that distracts from a focus on the God revealed in Jesus Christ is inappropriate. With that awareness though, on the whole, the more senses involved in receiving new information, the more engaged students are with the material, ensuring stronger storage in memory and increasing the likelihood that the information will be later retrieved and acted on. Although one should never use sensory involvement simply for the sake of using it, when it is included as part of an intentional design to reinforce the story, it can anchor that story in the mind of your congregants in ways lecture alone simply cannot. The medium actually is the message.

Lutheran pastor Bob Rognlien strongly believes in facilitating experiences that allow his congregation to experience God firsthand with the entire body, writing, "The time has come to transcend the contemporary worship trends of the late twentieth century and go beyond the calls for 'multisensory' or 'post-modern' worship in the early part of the twenty-first. We need worship that is thoroughly biblical, post-contemporary, pre-traditional—worship that leads us into a more complete encounter with God."[17] He contends that although God is to always be the focus of worship, it is the human experience that empowers our response to him.

---

[16] Charles Fadel and Cheryl Lemke, "Multimodal Learning Through Media: What the Research Says." *Meteri Group, Commissioned by Cisco Systems* (2008) http://www.cisco.com/ web/strategy/docs/education /Multimodal-Learning-Through-Media.pdf (accessed November 30, 2011).

[17] Bob Rognlien, *Experiential Worship: Encountering God with Heart, Soul, Mind, and Strength* (Colorado Springs, CO: NavPress, 2005), 25.

Chapter 8

MEMORY MAKING AND EMOTIONS

My husband Joe is a firefighter paramedic—a good one. He has a reputation for knowing what he is doing. He is one of the few who, while driving at breakneck speed to a call, has never had an accident in the ladder truck. He can start an IV in patients when no one else can even find a vein, much less hit it. He has the ability to calm frightened patients and family members as he remains emotionally detached during crisis situations—cool, calm, and collected. He never panics. Well, almost never.

While I was out of town for a few days Joe was taking care of our three daughters, ages eleven, nine, and six at the time. While working in his wood-shop, the girls were taking advantage of a textbook sunny day playing outdoors with their thirteen-year-old cousin and best friend, Jason. Knowing better than to divulge their plans to a responsible adult, our oldest daughter and Jason literally climbed out on a limb—a limb roughly twelve feet up a large tree overlooking an embankment. Once there, they tied a nylon rope around the limb above them and then proceeded to swing out into space 'Tarzan style.' As the oldest, Jason went first. He made it to the ground, both hands marked by rope burns but, nevertheless, in one piece. He then pulled the rope back to an undaunted Rachel, still perching high on a limb. Not to be outdone by the cousin she adored, Rachel grasped the rope and leaped from the tree, fully confident that she would gracefully arc through the air in a perfect parabola before doing an Olympic-worthy three-point landing. Instead, she lost her grip and landed on hard, solid ground.

Her sister Lauren rushed into the house to alert Joe that Rachel was seriously hurt. Knowing how children can exaggerate their scrapes and bruises, and without going to check for himself, Joe confidently assured Lauren that Rachel was fine. He then instructed her to tell Rachel to come inside so he could see what her problem was. Instead, Lauren burst into near-hysterical tears and began pulling her father toward the door. Joe reluctantly dropped what he was doing to walk with Lauren to the edge of the woods that bordered our property. There, he discovered his oldest daughter in extreme pain, her leg going in several different directions at once.

Joe had spent almost a decade responding to situations just like this. Broken bones were his stock and trade. If you are going to have a major accident, who better to have on hand than a trained, experienced paramedic? But Joe momentarily froze.

He stared at his daughter in openmouthed horror as an internal dialogue began running through his mind. An edited version may have looked something like this: *She's really hurt. I don't have time to make any mistakes. I've got to get this right the first time. What do I? Do I call the paramedics and wait on them to make the long trip to our home, or do I transport her to the hospital myself in my work van? Do I need to stay out here with her and comfort her, or do I leave that to her sisters and go inside to make some phone calls? Do I call her pediatrician and ask him to meet us at the hospital, or do I just rely on whatever doctor is already there? I know we have our pediatrician's phone number written down somewhere—but WHERE? And what do I do with Lauren, Joanna, and Jason while we're at the hospital? Maybe I should get a cold cloth to put on her head, or does she need ice packs for her leg before we leave?*

As his mind churned on and on, Rachel cried and Lauren and Joanna waited for him to *do something.* The good news is that they did eventually make it to the hospital. The bad news is that Rachel's leg was broken in three places, so she had to remain in the hospital for a several days.

During this crisis, Joe exhibited a trait common to all of us: It is impossible to separate thinking from feeling. Ever. No matter how logical you may think you are, your emotions have an immense influence on how you think, what you think, and what you do. Emotional involvement doesn't just happen during a crisis though. It's happening to a lesser degree all day, every day, influencing our understanding, our decisions, and our actions for better or for worse. Most of us can think of times when we have been so emotionally involved in something or with someone that we made regrettable decisions and serious mistakes.

More than any other factor, our emotional involvement (or lack thereof) determines if we pay attention to something, remember information, or take action on what we have learned.

Emotionally Motivated

We desperately want to believe that life makes sense, but it is humanly impossible to make sense of the enormous volume of information that assaults our senses daily. Because there is just too much to comprehend, early on our minds simply came to terms with the fact that all the material we take in is not equally beneficial. As it continuously sifts through sensory input (in an attempt to organize it in a meaningful way), it uses two rules of thumb to distinguish the significant from the not-so-significant material: (1) Is this information necessary for survival? (2) Does this information resonate with what I believe about life and who I believe I am? Without our ever realizing it, we are perpetually giving priority to those things that trigger our emotions.

In studying the absence of emotions in patients with prefrontal cortex damage, neuroscientist Antonio Damasio concluded, "There is a particular region in the human brain where the systems concerned with emotion/feeling, attention, and working memory interact so intimately that they constitute the source of energy of both external action (movement) and internal action (thought animation, reasoning)."[1] Damasio's research determined that when sensory data is routed to the brain, it merges with both emotions and intellect to become a unified whole. Even though the logical brain may establish our goals, it's the emotional brain that provides the enthusiasm to pursue those goals.

---

[1] Antonio Damasio, *Descartes' Error: Emotion, Reason, and the Human Brain* (New York: Penguin Books, 1994), 71.

Educational psychologist J. Diane Connell writes, "The emotional system tells us whether something is important—whether we ought to put energy or effort into it."[2]

Because emotions are, in fact, an instrumental part of the critical information we need to think logically, there is no need to fear their influence. Joddy Murray, Texas Christian's professor of rhetoric and composition, concurs. "Reason and affectivity are not inimical to one another; in fact, emotions make up what are often labeled as 'cool' or 'rational' affective states—intellectual interest or excitement, motivation, and concentration or attention are just three examples."[3] Jensen concedes that while it is possible for unrestrained emotion to severely impede rational thinking, "a lack of emotion can make for equally flawed thinking. . . . Students learn best when their minds, hearts, and bodies are engaged."[4]

Surprisingly, your emotions are not exclusively 'located' in your gray matter. Instead, they flow like a river throughout your body. "It's all done with an elaborate network of hormones and peptides, which influence thinking, moving, feeling, and decision-making. . . . The bottom line is that we are a complex system of systems, and the communication network does not consist solely of the neural networks; it's the bloodstream that supplies the chemical cocktail for the moment."[5]

All sensory information initially passes through the short-term memory for evaluation. Stolovich and Keeps state, "Short-term memory is like a buffer zone. It fills up rapidly and then quickly empties. This is due to a process known as endocytosis, which causes short-term memory to decay."[6] As sensory information is processed, if for some reason the emotions are activated, it is similar to a flashing red light signaling, "Stop! Pay attention! You need to remember this." This emotionally 'bookmarked' information is given highest priority and passed on to long-term memory. All other information is discarded.

---

[2] J. Diane Connell, "The Global Aspects of Brain-Based Learning," *Educational Horizons* 88, no. 1 (Fall 2009): 29.

[3] Murray, *Non-Discursive Rhetoric*, 104

[4] Jensen, *Brain-Based Learning*, 82.

[5] Jensen, *Brain-Based Learning*, 85

[6] Stolovich and Keeps, *Telling Ain't Training*, 25.

If you tend to think of long-term memory like a filing cabinet, you need to think again. Think less mechanically and more organically. Your long-term memory is similar to your circulatory system. Sensory information courses through your brain, your body, and your emotions. Jensen writes, "It is important to think process, rather than location, when discussing the memory system. The current understanding is that multiple memory locations and systems are responsible for our learning and recall."[7] He compares memory to a volunteer fire department that has no central headquarter. Instead, members in different locations are prepared to quickly respond to a call from several different sources and directions. The body, brain, and emotions are all recruited to recall information

When something is 'called to mind,' it is not just a cerebral event. Both your body and your emotions are also called to action. Memory is a whole-body event. There are some memories that can calm us, elicit laughter, or bring tears of joy to our eyes. Other memories can anger us, make our heart beat faster, or produce a knot in our stomach. We may discover ourselves blushing when a friend recounts an especially embarrassing incident in our past or cringing when we remember our eighth grade school photo.

Closely connected to the emotional significance of information is the usefulness of the information. If we see how information can be used in our daily life, it carries significantly more emotional weight. Thus, we are more likely to remember it and act on it. Again, this is because the brain is always operating in survival mode. It is constantly asking, "What's in this for me?" When something seems to have no immediate application, our mind considers it to be irrelevant and useless. It is not only easy to ignore; it's almost impossible to remember.

Any teacher who can help learners see the value of what is going to be taught beforehand will enhance the students' ability to remember. They are supplying the motivation for the learners to immediately incorporate newly acquired knowledge into their daily lives. The first Bible verse my mother ever taught me was Psalm 56:3: *When I am afraid, I will put my trust in you.* She taught it to the preschool me one day when the TV weatherman was predicting violent storms later that

---

[7] Jensen, *Brain-Based Learning*, 155.

Brain-Based Worship

evening. She informed me of the bad weather and told me that if I woke up and heard the thunder and wind that night, all I had to do was keep saying the verse and it would help me go back to sleep. Prepared in advance for the onslaught of a summer storm, I was given a powerful weapon with which to fight fear. Almost sixty years later, I still find myself repeating it an all kinds of situations.

Manipulation or Motivation?

Granted, no teacher can control the emotions of the learners, nor should they even try to do so. They can, however, strongly influence their mindsets through the atmosphere and arrangement of the learning environment and the presentation of material. Keep in mind that there is a huge difference between manipulating the emotions and engaging the emotions in a safe and challenging environment. Emotional manipulation is always unethical, be it in classroom or sanctuary.

Emotionally manipulative people have but one goal—to get what they want, when they want it, the way they want it. In short, they manipulate others for their own benefit and personal gain by using unethical means to attain what appears (to them) to be a good end. In an attempt to eliminate any legitimate resistance to what they think they need, they will deliberately attempt to undermine the decision-making processes of individuals and groups. They may try to make others feel indebted to them by using flattery, or they may resort to deceit, blame, and guilt to control the actions of others. Instead of genuinely listening, they will tell others what they are 'supposed to feel.' If anyone should disagree with them, they will go on the offensive, acting as if their integrity has been challenged. The manipulator may be completely aware of what they are doing. On the other hand, they may have no awareness of the fact that they are playing dirty.

Because we humans can be so blissfully unaware of our own motivation, it is important for teachers and leaders to regularly and persistently examine ourselves in this area—asking ourselves if we could possibly be using illegitimate means to reach a legitimate end. Are we empowering those with whom we work to make better decisions for themselves or are we telling them what to think and how to act? Are we using flattery or guilt to push them in a direction we prefer? Do we allow them to express negative emotions without denigrating those feelings or trying to correct them? Asking these questions can help us distinguish between using emotions to manipulate a group and using emotions to facilitate learning. When used to expedite learning, emotions are a valuable tool that serves to anchor learning to the soul.

Implications for Worship

Ever since the Enlightenment, we pastors have been trained to preach carefully constructed analytical sermons that appeal to the mind. In a further attempt to appear relentlessly rational, we may avoid expressing strong emotion in worship. Following that lead, our congregants will keep emotions reined in until what they believe is a more appropriate time. As a result, few twenty-first century worshippers have regular opportunities to create emotionally anchored, God-moment memories.

When Methodism was experiencing its fastest growth, her pastors were unafraid of showing emotional intensity. Congregants followed their lead, thus earning early Methodists the derisive designation *enthusiasts*. Those who mocked her eagerness to worship learned to their regret that passion was attractive. It still is. The fastest growing Christian communities around the world today are those Pentecostal communities that express unrestrained emotional involvement with Jesus Christ.

No one, absolutely no one, has more to get excited about than those who grasp God's abiding love for His creation and his creatures. If we are not communicating that love with unreserved enthusiasm, why should the world bother to take us seriously? The two pilgrims on the Emmaus Road were able to communicate the gospel effectively to the disciples because they were enthusiastically and emotionally involved with Jesus. *Were not our hearts burning within us while he talked with us on the road and opened the Scriptures to us?* (Luke 24:32). They were thrilled to be walking with Jesus, bubbling over with elation as they shared the news with others, grinning like children on Christmas morning.

It is not inherently manipulative when a teacher speaks passionately about a subject. I learned to love history because William Clayton Wright was a passionate teacher of said subject. He did not try to tone his mannerism down to appear more dignified and cerebral. Instead, he just 'let it fly.' His love for the discipline radiated from his very being. I cannot honestly say that I retain all the content of his teaching, but because I did catch his enthusiasm, even today I have a fair grasp on the endless stream of history. Learning is contagious. We always tend catch what our teachers are most excited about.

It is only natural to grow more emphatic in tone and gesture when we are enthusiastic about something. This is not manipulation; it is honesty, pure and simple. For those who adore the risen Christ, it amounts to being authentic. Young adults today crave and respond to authenticity in their mentors, but be warned: Trying to mimic a passion that does not exist is ill advised. Your congregation will see through the hypocrisy and be repulsed. It is better to be honest about the fact that we ministers also struggle with faith, that there are days when we carry such heavy doubts that we feel it physically, that on occasion we have to force ourselves to get behind the pulpit. Your people need to hear that at times. It gives them hope for their own faltering faith. Logic may tell you to do otherwise. It will try to convince you that your church needs an invulnerable super-hero of a leader to emulate—but even Jesus allowed himself to be vulnerable and express doubt. We would be foolish to hold ourselves to a higher standard than his.

Remember that although logic may appear impressive on academic papers, it is not memorable. That's because memory is not something that happens in the brain; it happens throughout the body. Accordingly, it is past time to forego sermons designed for the intellect and instead preach to the entire body—head, heart, and gut—the combination of which almost guarantees retention.

When it comes to the "What's in it for me?" question, any churchgoer who dared to verbalize it would probably be castigated. Admittedly, on the surface, it does seem utterly self-centered. In truth, asking the question is part of being human. Christians ask it just as often as everyone else. We just don't like to admit it. Until we recognize this reality, we will be unable to deal with our own motivation.

With maturation and sound instruction, the Christian grows to understand that the payoff for a follower of Jesus is to be more fully transformed into his image. Our job is to communicate to our listeners that the 'benefits' of following Jesus look more like the fruits of the Spirit than the fruits of culturally defined 'success.' Encouraging our congregation members to ask, "What's in it for me?" can help them come to terms with selfish motivation while they develop the skills to maximize their own potential as Christ followers. They may also grow in the awareness that salvation is about so much more than where they spend eternity. It's about finding a calmness of spirit in this lifetime that enables us to live our lives without regret.

Chapter 9

Storied Memory

By the time Jacob entered fourth grade, he was intimately acquainted with failure. Having barely made it through his first three years of elementary school, he was decidedly less than enthusiastic about yet another year of academia.

In Alabama, fourth grade marks the time when every student is required to study Alabama history. During our initial parent-teacher conference, Jacob's mother expressed her concern that history would be his downfall, stating, "He doesn't do well with dates. He barely remembers his own birthday. How will he ever 'Remember the Alamo'––or the Battle of Horseshoe Bend, or The Montgomery Bus Boycott? He'll never pass history."

I explained to her that with a few big exceptions, he would not be memorizing dates. I was infinitely more interested in my students learning the flow and connection of events than having them pinpoint exact dates, so I taught history as story.

Jacob seemed to respond well to this method. He paid close attention during class as I told the stories of the early explorers. He grew outraged by their flagrant abuse of Alabama's Native Americans. He became incensed when we took a look at slavery. He understood the strategic importance of Mobile Bay. He asked questions, completed reading assignments, and participated in related activities with considerably more ease than he did in any other subject.

One morning in November, I noticed that this normally energetic and rambunctious boy was surprisingly quiet. He appeared tired and flushed. When I asked if he was feeling sick, he assured me that he was fine. As the morning went on though, he continued to wilt. Finally, I laid my hand on his forehead to discover that he was burning up with fever.

I looked him in the eyes and said, "Jacob. You're sick and you're going home. I'm calling your mother right now."

Jacob responded with an almost panicked, "No! Please don't make me go home!"

Surprised by this unexpected, one-in-ten-thousand reaction, I asked, "Why not?" Jacob hung his head as if in shame and mumbled, "I knew I was sick when I woke up this morning, but I didn't tell Mom." He then spoke the words that thrilled me to the core. "I couldn't miss school today. I have to find out what happens next in Alabama history. Can't we wait until after history to call Mom?"

Story Magic

Good stories are strong magic. The right story can bring a rampaging three year-old to a halt, stir a hardened adult to tears, lower blood pressure, awaken a spirit of generosity, or help someone come face-to-face with his or herself. The wrong story can lead to prejudice, aggression, war—even genocide.

In the 19th century, the doctrine of *Manifest Destiny*—the widely held belief that Americans were destined to expand across the North America continent and redeem the savage West—was accepted by her citizens as if it were official governmental policy. It was not. It was a storyline, but when this idea was planted in the American mind, along with the then-popular and grandiose notions of American exceptionalism and Romantic nationalism, the American people swallowed it hook, line, and sinker. In doing so, they adopted a new identity—that of a people destined by God to be an imperial power with a mission to remake the world in the image of the United States. This new 'story' about who the country was as a nation set the stage and gave divine rationalization to a series of bloody wars.

There is no longer any doubt that stories create our world. We understand who we are through the stories we hear and believe. When our background story is absent, as in the case of an adopted child, we will often go to great lengths to learn it. Author Patrick J. Lewis writes, "Without a story, there is no identity, no self, no other."[1] Leonard Sweet observes, "Like heat-seeking missiles, humans are story-seeking creatures."[2] Our mind is attracted to a gripping story like a sunflower is attracted to the sun. The thirst for story is built into us. So just why are stories so irresistible and compelling? How do they cast their semi-supernatural spell?

As explained in chapter 6, the brain of every living creature is focused on one thing: survival. Alert for any kind of threat, it never stops surveying the environment. Relentlessly bombarded by sensory information, the brain is capable of taking in 11,000,000 pieces of information *each second*. Of those, it consciously registers 'only' about forty. In the end, it processes between three and seven per second.

It can only deal with this massive influx because the brain has no central command post. Instead, it has millions of highly localized processors distributed throughout, constantly taking readings of surroundings while simultaneously communicating with each other. These neural processors rapidly sift through sensory information, examining it for anything that might affect physical, emotional, or social survival. While doing so, the processors also search for patterns in that information—especially cause and effect patterns.

After filtering out all unnecessary sensory information, the brain judges the significance of the retained material, theorizing how it might affect us. Finally, trying to make all the data understandable, it assigns meaning to the information in story form. It does this so naturally and so subtly that we are seldom aware that it's happening. Without our conscious awareness, the brain writes a script to make the information more memorable, easier to communicate to others, and more convincing.

---

[1] Patrick J. Lewis, "Storytelling as Research/Research as Storytelling," *Qualitative Inquiry* 17, no. 6 (2011): 505. http://qix.sagepub.com/content/17/6/505 (accessed November 24, 2012).

[2] Leonard Sweet, "Storytellers Change the World: A Film Review of 'Lincoln,'" *Beyond Evangelical: The Blog of Frank Viola*, entry posted December 7, 2012. http://frankviola.org/2012/12/07/lincoln (accessed December 7, 2012).

For example, if you discover a dented left side-panel on your automobile after it has been parked all day long in your normal space at your place of employment, your mind will begin to formulate an explanation for the damage that may sound something like this: *Bob always parks his car in the place beside me, but not today. I don't see it anywhere. Bob was at work today—but he came in five minutes late. He never does that. He must have clipped my car pulling in this morning. When he realized that no one saw him do it, he probably moved his car to a different area of the parking lot hoping I wouldn't put two and two together. That jerk is trying to avoid a repair bill!"* This explanation may have absolutely nothing to do with reality, but because your mind frantically needs a story to explain the event, it will create one (or several) to do so.

The more logical left-hemisphere of the brain is responsible for taking all the information deemed pertinent and searching for a *why* behind it. It does this by merging it together, interpreting it, and coming up with a baseline explanation for the known facts in story form. Literary scholar Jonathan Gottschall explains, "The left-brain is a classic know-it-all; when it doesn't know the answer to a question, it can't bear to admit it. . . . It would rather fabricate a story than leave something unexplained."[3]

We are so driven to derive meaning that we will impose meaning when it does not exist. By failing to distinguish between what we know for a fact and what we assume, we humans often jump to erroneous conclusions. This explains why people can claim to see Jesus on a piece of cheese toast, perceive animals in cumulus cloud formations, swear by a 'lucky' shirt, or believe that any team that makes the cover of Sports Illustrated is jinxed. It also explains conspiracy theories. The need to make sense out of random information is so strong that it continues even as we sleep. Dreams are simply stories the brain tells itself to help it deal with important information ignored during waking hours.

As soon as the left-brain begins to create and structure a story with "Once upon a time," it engages the more creative right brain to supplement that story with details. The right brain simply accepts the

---

[3] Jonathan Gottschall, *The Storytelling Animal: How Stories Make Us Human* (Boston: Houghton Mifflin Harcourt, 2012), 99.

left-brain's imposed structure as a scaffolding to build upon, adding an entire realm of specifics to it based on the unconscious information we carry from past experiences. Thus, the right brain contributes the supplemental sensory information needed to conjure up imaginary scenarios, settings, landscapes, sounds, and images. This allows us to visualize someone's appearance, attribute characteristics to them, even concoct emotions, thoughts, and preferences for them. Story practitioner Dr. Juliet Bruce writes, "Very briefly, story channels the intuitive, emotional, and inspired power of your right brain through the rational, structuring left brain. Aligned, the two hemispheres of your brain exert an enormous integrating and creative power, very likely beyond anything you've experienced."[4]

As the bits and pieces come together in a coherent, logical story, our brain is rewarded with a firing of dopamine neurons. Dopamine is the neurotransmitter that controls the brain's reward and pleasure centers, regulates movement and emotional response, and enables us not only to see future rewards, but also to take action to move toward them. Even when our conclusions are embarrassingly incorrect, we are actually rewarded with a feeling of pleasure for supposedly figuring out what is going on.

Shaped By Story

Not only are we wired to create stories, we are wired to receive stories. Listening to a story is never a passive act. From the moment someone begins to tell a story, our mind churns, looking for a reason to care about the story, for the meaning behind it, and for what is at stake. Unconsciously, we probe the teller's words for significance. If we don't begin to find meaning almost immediately, we tune out. If we do find meaning, the story can seize our attention and refuse to let us go.

Why does a good story grip us? It allows us to live vicariously. Even though we don't want to undergo conflict or danger in real life, we still

---

[4] Juliet Bruce, Ph.D. "This is Your Brain on Story." *Living Story Blogspot*, entry posted January 15, 2012. http://livingstory-ny.blogspot.com/2012/01/this-is-your-brain-on-story-html (accessed September 13, 2012).

need to know how to deal with it. While absorbed in a story, we can experience the conflict we fear and develop some very real skills for handling it. Bruce observes, "We get to try on trouble, pretty much risk-free."[5] In Gottschall's words, "Like a flight simulator, fiction projects us into intense simulations of problems that run parallel to those we face in reality. We have a rich experience and we don't die in the end. Fiction is an ancient virtual reality technology that specializes in simulating human problems."[6]

Years later, even if we barely remember a story, the implicit wisdom couched in the story is still accessible to our mind if we need it. Geoff Kaufmann and Lisa Libby, professors of psychology at Ohio State, write, "In a very real sense, people who have read good literature have lived more than people who cannot or will not read. It is not true that we have only one life to lead; if we can read, we can live as many more lives and as many kind of lives as we wish."[7]

While our mind is searching for meaning in a story, it is also visualizing meaning. The majority of any story takes place in our own imagination. With only a hint of direction from the storyteller, "Our minds supply most of the information in a scene—most of the color, shading, and texture. . . .The writer guides the way we imagine but does not determine it."[8] For example, in the act of reading the phrase 'It was a dark and stormy night,' our mind begins to construct mental images—landscape, trees, buildings, and starless skies. Those mental images emerge without our conscious awareness, carrying a sort of physical concreteness that exceeds any information provided by the storyteller.

Why? Research indicates the existence of mirror neurons—neurons that fire both when we do something and when we observe someone else do the same thing. Predictably, mirror neurons fire more frequently

---

[5] Lisa Cron, *Wired for Story: The Writer's Guide to Using Brain Science to Hook Readers from the Very First Sentence* (New York: Ten Speed Press, 2012), 126.

[6] Gottschall, *The Storytelling Animal*, 58-59.

[7] Geoff F. Kaufman and Lisa K. Libby, "Changing Beliefs and Behavior Through Experience-Taking." *Journal of Personality and Social Psychology* 103, no. 1 (2012): 1. http://ncbi.nlm.nih.gov/pubmed/22448888 (accessed November 20, 2012).

[8] Gottschall, *The Storytelling Animal*, 5.

during emotional responses. For example, if we drop our steak knife and must bend over to pick it up, very few neurons will fire. If we have a steak knife thrown at us, there is an explosion of neurons because in this case our emotions are involved. If we observe someone drop their steak knife, few neurons will fire in our brain. If we witness a steak knife thrown at the same person, so many neurons will fire that we find ourselves flinching along with the one targeted.

If you witness a marriage proposal that is enthusiastically accepted, you feel a bit of joy yourself. When your team wins the Super Bowl, you feel the same joy the players feel. When Pharrell Williams sings "Happy," you find yourself feeling happier. Mirror neurons enable you to feel what others experience as if you are personally experiencing it. "By reflecting the actions of others in our own brains, mirror neurons may enable us to feel empathy, to intuit other people's emotions, and to guess other people's motivations. Mirror neurons may be the neurological shoehorn that allows us to slip into other people's shoes."[9]

Amazingly, you don't just mirror flesh-and-blood people; you also mirror characters in stories. In a study at Washington University in which individuals read or heard short stories while undergoing MRIs of the brain, it was discovered that "the areas of the brain that lit up when they read about an activity were identical to those that light up when they actually did the activity."[10] The same areas of the brain that process sensory information in real life are activated whenever you listen to a compelling story.

Your mind responds as if you are actually experiencing the events described in a story. You mentally participate in the narrative, experiencing the story viscerally—not quite as intensely as you would if the story was actually happening to you, but it does affect you. Are you doubtful? Think about the last horror movie you watched. Even though you intellectually knew that you were in no danger, at some point you probably found yourself cringing, gasping, or screaming along with the characters on the big screen.

---

[9] James Geary, *I Is an Other: The Secret Life of Metaphor and How It Shapes the Way We See the World* (New York: HarperCollins, 2011), 53.

[10] Cron, *Wired for Story*, 67.

You react physically to stories—laughing, crying, cringing, muscles tensing, and respiration increasing during anxious moments. The story actually changes your physiology. Research shows that while watching fight scenes, a viewer's testosterone level increases as much as thirty percent. This is true of both sexes. Similarly, while absorbed in a romantic 'chick flick,' there was a ten percent increase in progesterone levels.[11]

A story not only changes your physiology, it also changes your emotions. You always experience a story emotionally. In one study, subjects in an MRI scanner were screened as they watched a film of an actor drinking from a cup and then grimacing in disgust, as they listened to a story about accidently bumping into a vomiting drunk and catching some of the vomit in their own mouths, and as they actually tasted a disgusting solution for themselves. In all three cases, the anterior insula—the seat of disgust—lit up as if the scenarios were actually happening to them.[12]

An emotional story activates the hormone oxytocin, helping you feel empathy and bond with others so you can step out of your own shoes and see the world differently. In one study, "Getting volunteers to watch a 5-minute video telling the story of a four-year-old boy with terminal brain cancer increased oxytocin levels by an average of 47% compared with others who watched an emotionally neutral film about the same boy going to the zoo."[13] A neutral story is not memorable because it bores you, even distracts you from learning. Emotional content is what hooks you to a story. If you are not feeling the story, you have no reason to care about the outcome. When you do resonate emotionally with a story, it is similar to remembering a vivid event that is actually happening to you. Good stories literally get inside your head—and your body.

---

[11] Jennifer Williams, "Your Brain on Stories." *Verillance (n) Truth and Brilliance, Better Marketing Through Science*, entry posted February 28, 2011, http://www.verilliance.com/2011/02/28/your-brain-on-stories/ (accessed November 3, 2012).

[12] Gottschall, *The Storytelling Animal*, 62-63.

[13] Williams, "Your Brain on Stories."

Connected by Story

Historically, stories have been used to transmit the values of the storyteller to the listener. The closer the relationship between the teller and the hearer, the greater the possibility that values will be transmitted. The stories that parents tell to their children nearly always convey right and wrong, good and evil. As children listen to them, they learn what culture expects from them. Stories convey such lessons as "Don't be too fast jumping to conclusions" (*Chicken Little*), "Don't give up when something is difficult" (*The Little Engine that Could*), or "Don't talk to strangers" (*Little Red Riding Hood*). When I discovered I was pregnant, the first thing I did was rush to a bookstore and purchase a copy of *The Velveteen Rabbit* for my yet-to-be child. I wanted him or her to learn the lessons the little rabbit learned the hard way—and I didn't want them to have to wait until their *eyes fell out* and *most of their hair was loved off*. As parents tell or read stories to their children, they are, in fact, narrating ways of being.

Knowing our own story is vital to knowing who we are. Parents who tell their children the story of their family assist the child in developing a strong identity, but it's not just children who want to know where they came from. The web site Ancestry.com operates a network of genealogical and historical record websites. At last count, more than two million story-hungry subscribers have been willing to pay for the service. Even when we know who our immediate relatives are, we want to know the rest of our story. From what country(s) did our ancestors come? What values did their family promote? Did anyone ever blaze a trail to a new land or a new endeavor? Who were the veterans, the educated ones, the horse thieves, the farmers, the shopkeepers, or the blacksmiths?

Most adults like to imagine that, unlike children, they are too intelligent to have their mind 'infected' by a story, yet in a 2009 study, seventy-five percent of people who viewed a disturbing horror movie admitted to later having intense anxiety, disruptive thoughts, and sleeplessness. For a quarter of those subjects, the effects lingered years after the movie was over. The movie *Psycho* brought decades of shower anxiety to some, while the movie *Jaws* has never entirely released the general public from the grip of fear. Some of the original viewers still contend with memories that keep them out of the water. For good or for bad, the stories that rivet our attention change us.

Bonded by Story

Good stories build community by creating emotional connections. They can unite an audience composed of individuals who otherwise have nothing in common. For instance, I went to see "Schindler's List" as soon as it came out in theaters. That night, as the viewers arrived at the screening, they exhibited the entire range of human interaction—laughing, arguing, engaging in nervous banter, speaking loudly (or softly) about their day. Three hours later, everyone—absolutely everyone—left the theater united in total silence. The story had been emotionally contagious, choreographing both our thoughts and our behavior. Overwhelmed by the horror of it all, none of us could deal with more trivial conversation.

Storytelling has always served to bind societies together by reinforcing the values of the community. In this country for instance, we train our children to be good citizens not by teaching them the rules of our land but by telling stories about national heroes: George Washington, incapable of telling a lie; Abraham Lincoln walking six miles through snow to return a few cents he overcharged a customer while working at a dry-goods store; Harriet Tubman working as a conductor on the underground railroad. Those stories are continually reinforced throughout life as we celebrate national holidays. As I write this, our country is observing Veterans' Day. Every newscast and several children's shows have told at least part of the story of how this holiday came to be. The same will happen on MLK's birthday, President's Day, Independence Day, and Thanksgiving. Our shared stories cement us together. Gottschall rightly observes, "Story—sacred and profane—is perhaps the main cohering force in human life."[14]

Even as an individual reads or watches a story alone, they are still being defined communally. The story is instilling cultural values in all

---

[14] Gottschall, *The Storytelling Animal*, 138.

who hear it. While watching *The Patriot,* even those who lean decidedly toward pacifism find it almost impossible not to root for violent rebellion. *The Lorax* will have the audience questioning unrestrained capitalism and wanting to be a better steward of creation. *Rudy* will convince them that they can surmount any obstacle if they try hard enough. Marketing and design specialist Nancy Duarte correctly writes, "Stories are the most powerful delivery tool for information, more powerful and more enduring than any other art form. . . . Information is static. Stories are dynamic. . . . Stories link one person's heart to another."[15]

Even as we listen to or read the news, we are being formed by the stories we hear. For that reason, it is wise to remember that news outlets have their own agendas. Different news channels tell the same stories with decidedly different slants and emphases. They build and reinforce allegiance to their particular opinion or ideology using the most powerful of all opinion makers: story.

Repairing Broken Presentations

More than anything else, story creates a climate of change, verbally generating a collective resonance that can transform an audience. Marketers understand this and use it. The always highly anticipated Super Bowl advertisements are nearly all in story form. A mini-Darth Vader using *The Force* to magically start a Volkswagen, Dodge's heart-tugging *God Made a Farmer*, the ongoing tale of Budweiser's Clydesdales, or Audi's unforgettable *Prom* commercial—all are short stories that captured a nation's attention. Even though air-time to tell these stories cost an average of four million dollars for thirty seconds, the advertisers believe the cost would be higher not to tell them—catastrophic even. The stories gave the companies an identity that people would remember and to which they would return.

The purpose of all teaching—in the classroom, the boardroom, or the sanctuary—is to induce changed thought and behavior in the learner. This goal can be difficult to achieve because the brain, always

---

[15] Nancy Duarte, *Resonate: Present Visual Stories That Transform Audiences* (Hoboken, NJ: Wiley, 2010), 16.

more cautious in new and unfamiliar situations, views change as a huge threat. Getting someone to commit to change is always a challenge. Fortunately, even though we are wired to resist change, stories have the ability to tap deeply into our emotions like few other things can, thus making stories powerful change agents.

The emotional conflict at the heart of every good story allows the hearer to understand that 'all is not as it seems,' that things could be better, that some kind of 'change' could bring vast improvement to a situation. TV's Dr. Phil McGraw uses this tactic when he invites his guests to tell their own stories of dysfunction and then asks, "Well, how's that working for you?" He is allowing their own account of their messed-up life to jump-start the process of change, facilitating the knowledge that there is a difference between 'what is' and 'what could be.'

Stories expose a gap between the here-and-now and prospects for a better future by juxtaposing actuality with possibility. The storyteller who lays down a baseline mental image of the existing world followed by a starkly contrasting image of what 'could be' throws the audience off balance. Once the hearer understands what's at stake, they begin to mull over possible solutions to the conflict being described. For devising those potential solutions, they are rewarded with a delightful dopamine rush. Once the rush begins, it can be almost impossible to pull away from the story.

Have you ever wondered why countless people stood in line at the bookstore for hours to buy the final *Harry Potter* installment? Or why others slept on the sidewalk so they could be in the first screening of *Star Wars: Episode 1*? What is the new phenomena of TV bing-watching all about? And who hasn't sat through the last thirty minutes of a good movie in utter misery because they could not imagine taking a restroom break and missing something important?

Good stories are just plain addictive. Even if a story makes the hearer uncomfortable, if it produces even a modicum of curiosity, he or she will likely continue to listen to it and thus consider alternative scenarios. Stories shove the hearer out of comfortable complacency and into action. They extend a call to adventure that allows the storyteller to plant invisible but disruptive seeds in the fertile soil of the imagination, seeds of change that can take root and turn lives and communities upside down.

Writer and graphic designer Nancy Duarte explains that we usually move too fast when expecting people to make changes. "The audience needs to change on the inside before they can change on the outside."[16] Inner change is instigated by a spellbinding story that sets up the possibility of a different future, allowing the hearer to imagine ways to bring that future about. Only after that inner change is made can the storyteller call for outer change.

Duarte points out that because humans have such different personalities and temperaments, there are four types of outer change (or responses) to emphasize in every group. Audiences consist of *doers* who gladly instigate activities, *suppliers* who provide resources, *influencers* who can sway the opinions of others, and *innovators* who generate ideas and create strategies. An appeal for action should address each of these groups. The audience needs to understand that all four responses are needed if the imagined dream for a better future is to come true.

Do not, however, make the mistake of ending with the appeal for change, because the audience will remember the last thing they hear more vividly than anything else—and the last thing they hear needs to engage the emotions. For this reason, always end with a compelling takeaway in the form of a vivid image of what can be if action is taken. Conclude *not* by offering ways to apply the lessons but by describing how the world will be different if and when the modifications are made.

The use of story allows for three-way interaction between the audience, the storyteller, and the story. The storyteller interacts with their audience verbally and non-verbally using eye contact, gesture, and tone of voice to convey their message and create strong visual images. They interact with the story as they adjust it to emphasize different things to different audiences.

The listeners, too, interact with the story. Considering that we live in a day when audiences demand interactive participation, this is crucial. When a story has authenticity, coherence, and integrity, it unleashes creativity and invites maximum engagement of the mind. The listeners participate by constructing meaning. Because the mind wants to make meaning for itself,

---

[16] Duarte, *Resonate,* 32.

it is a mistake to explicitly tell the hearers what they should take away from the story. The listeners also participate by signaling cues of acceptance or rejection, allowing the storyteller to adjust the presentation if needed.

As the listeners interact with the story, they are mentally unpacking it. They are figuring out what it means for them personally, struggling with inner conflict, relationship issues, expectations, rivalries, meaning, and choices. Without even knowing it, they are forming a narrative about themselves as they listen—who they are, why they exist, how they relate to others, and what they value.

Because today's best educators are acutely aware of the power of story, they are exploiting it as a means to capture attention, motivate, build memory, stimulate inquiry, develop critical thinking skills, develop emotional IQ, transmit values, and build social skills. Because they also understand that the impact of a story increases exponentially when it is enabled to flow across multiple neural pathways, they supplement those stories with images, tastes, smells, sounds, and related activities. More than ever, educators are using multi-media storytelling methods, connecting still images, sounds, texts, video clips, smells, interactive dialogue and more. In the words of Pamela Rutledge, Director of the Media Psychology Research Center, we can weave together "individual strands of a story into a larger and richer interactive fabric that offers the audience multiple opportunities to participate, through content production, collaboration, and interaction."[17] Each form of media used during a presentation contributes a distinct element to the narrative, creating a holistic experience for the audience that is satisfying, meaningful, and, potentially, transformational.

Telling Stories in Church

Too many ministers are convinced that their sermons should be relentlessly logical. Writing a sermon as if they were writing an

---

[17] Pamela Rutledge, "Transmedia Storytelling: The Reemergence of Fundamentals," *Psychology Today* (January 7, 2011). http://www.psychologytoday.com/blog/positively-media/201101/transmedia-storytelling-the-reemergence-fundamentals (accessed November 3, 2012).

academic paper on what factors led to U.S. involvement in World War II, they carefully outline points and sub-points to shore up an argument. They carefully avoid highly emotional content, convinced that it is impossible to be emotional and logical at the same time. Leonard Sweet rightly observes, "We treat God as an entity to be discussed and debated at our peril. God is primarily to be experienced and worshipped, not some object of speculation but a subject of adoration and relationship. The God of Abraham, Deborah, David, and Jesus is a *with* God, not an *about* God."[18] If we make a worship service *about* God, we have failed. If we believe that the more information *about* God we can pack into a sermon the greater the chance the sermon will effect change, we have failed. A successful worship service is a service that paves the way for people to meet *with* God.

It is completely possible to remain true to facts while creating necessary emotional appeal using story. Could the story of Joseph being sold as a slave by his brothers be any more emotional? Can you even begin to imagine Adam's response the first time he saw Eve? What about Hagar's fear and confusion upon being abandoned with her son in the wilderness? Or how much frustration did Jesus feel when he repeatedly had to teach the same lesson to his disciples? Leonard Sweet points out that there is a good reason his followers were called "Duh-ciples."

To tell the story well, one must first know the story. This begins with understanding the meta-narrative, or overarching story of Scripture. The Bible is not just a collection of random, loosely related stories. It is one story, a big story conveyed by God to reveal himself to humanity, a story that culminates with his incarnation. Everything that came before Jesus pointed to him. Everything that came after Jesus comes from him. There is a unity in the story that is too often ignored or unrecognized.[19] The preacher should strive to relate each week's sermon to the big picture of God's love for humanity.

As you plan for each worship service, soak yourself in the story you will be telling. Read through it multiple times using different

---

[18] Leonard Sweet, Facebook, June 15, 2014.

[19] For an excellent book that gives attention to on the metanarrative of Scripture, see: Leonard I. Sweet and Frank Viola, *Jesus: A Theography* (Nashville, TN: Thomas Nelson, 2012).

translations. Imagine what each character may be feeling, fearing, thinking, or avoiding. Don't be afraid to go there. Emotions are the driving force behind all our actions. They cause us to care about an issue or topic. Because we seldom act by reason alone, we rarely make major changes in life based strictly on accurate information. No matter how accurate the information may be, if it is without emotional impact, it bores us.

Keep in mind that the God who speaks in Scripture is a storytelling God who conveyed the most basic and timeless information about who we are and who he is through the creation stories of Genesis. He gifted Israel with her identity using the stories of Abraham, Isaac, and Jacob. The establishment of the covenant was given not as part of a legal document but as part of the Exodus story. Nathan used a story to force David to confront some very unflattering truths about himself. Amos told short stories to communicate God's pending judgment on Israel. The story of Jonah is a comedy of biblical proportions—a self-righteous prophet of God who ran from the very God he claimed to love and ended up with what can only be called a suspiciously fishy rededication to his task.

Jesus himself, a peerless storyteller, used story as his primary teaching tool. At no point did he give his followers a list of things they had to believe, an inventory of behaviors they needed to adopt or abandon, or a three-point sermon. Instead, he told stories that connected to his audience's everyday lives and their imaginations. Only on one occasion did he explain the meaning of a story.[20] Perhaps that is one reason people flocked to him instead of the other teachers of his day.

The church was birthed in the midst of narrative as Peter told the story of Jesus to the masses. In the stories of Lydia, Philip, and Cornelius, listeners learn how the church spread like wildfire as people told the Jesus story. The stories of Paul teach what it means to be *faithful*. The story of Stephen, martyred while telling a story, demonstrates just how dangerous a well-told story can be.

If our world seems to be going crazy, it's because the wrong stories are being told. The shape of our transformation greatly depends on what stories we hear—yet a deplorable number of 'churched' individuals never hear the stories of Scripture. As a whole, the church is failing to

---

[20] Matthew 13:1–18

tell God's life-shaping, priority changing, grace soaked stories. Even our most committed church members are receiving their self-definition from the stories told in movies, on TV, and through advertisements. It is vital that they be intimately acquainted with the stories of faith if they have any hope of living lives of faith. Those stories will circumscribe how they think, what they do, and who they are.

In spite of diligent effort on our part to communicate the Gospel, ministers of all faiths find themselves frustrated by lack of noticeable transformation in the lives of congregants. Perhaps this is in large part because we have neglected the most valuable tool we have for facilitating transformation. Humans were wired from day one to respond to story, but when was the last time you told or heard a biblical story told—beginning to end—from the pulpit? How much time during worship is devoted to telling those stories?

The norm for the North American pastor continues to be the propositional sermons. Instead of telling the stories, we slice and dice the biblical narrative into steps and rules: *Four Steps to a Better Marriage, Five Ways to Pray, How to Forgive Yourself,* ad infinitum. We strip the life from the story and substitute rules, plans, proposals, and applications—all of which generate conformity, not transformation. They also generate boredom.

We pastors preach propositionally for several reasons. Most of us were taught to preach that way in seminary. In addition, we preach like our role models—who also were taught to preach propositionally. We may even feel pressured to demonstrate our hard-earned academic knowledge, but Truth is never recognized in dry academia or dusty data. Truth is recognized relationally. From beginning to end, Scripture is a story of relationship—relationship with God and with others as embodied in Jesus Christ. We need to return to that embodied, incarnated story.

It may be difficult for us to admit to ourselves, but no one cares how perfectly outlined our sermons are. No one cares if we have three alliterated points with a logical conclusion. No one cares whether our oratory is more Calvinistic or Armenian. Few even care if we view baptism as symbolic of death and resurrection or as cleansing. On the other hand, they care deeply about whether they hear from God.

To successfully navigate through life, our congregants need more than a litany of propositions; they need the Divine wisdom that comes only through personally wrestling with the emotionally gripping, anything-but-boring stories of Scripture. The wisdom and skills needed to follow Jesus are buried in those stories. Our task is to help our congregants mine those truths for all they are worth.

When King Josiah allowed the long-silent word of God to speak for itself, God breathed new life into it, and a nation was transformed. It is time for us to do the same. It is time to allow God to speak through biblical stories and trust that when his Word goes out, it will not return empty, but will accomplish what he desires and achieve the purpose for which he sent it. (Isaiah 55:11)

Reformed theologian James K.A. Smith writes, "We live into the stories we've absorbed; we become characters in the drama that has captivated us. Thus, much of our action is acting out a kind of script that has unconsciously captured our imagination."[21] As worship leaders, our job is to tell God's stories in ways that captivate. Transformational learning will occur as we return our focus to the story of the God who reveals himself to us through his Living Word and his written word.

The narratives of Scripture naturally lend themselves to spurring transformation because they are stories of failure, despair, betrayal, second chances, hope, redemption, and new life. Because every story in the Bible glimmers with hope for a day yet to come, every sermon should include hope for a different and better future. Your people will be primed to open themselves to the transforming work of the Spirit when they hear God's narrative told in memorable, impassioned, heart-gripping ways. If you supplement those biblical stories with the stories of faithful individuals and groups in your church, with appropriate images, with multi-sensory activities, and with choices offered in a safe atmosphere, their impact grows exponentially. As your listeners examine their own story in the light of God's story, they are in fact rewriting their story as a chapter in the grand narrative of God. Pastors who tell God's stories are privileged to serve as guides in the process of transformation and healing.

---

[21] James K A. Smith, *Imagining the Kingdom: How Worship Works* (*Cultural Liturgies*, vol. 2), Grand Rapids, MI: Baker Academic, 2013), 32.

Chapter 10

METAPHORICAL MEMORY

There was nothing 'soft' or 'forgiving' about the golf-ball-sized chunk of granite handed to each person entering the sanctuary. With no explanation as to why they were receiving the hefty rocks, they accepted the stones with puzzled expressions. Their attention, however, shifted away from the curious souvenir as soon as the service began. By the time the sermon started, the rocks were all but forgotten.

The text was Luke 6:27–37; the subject was forgiveness. I began by speaking of the universal struggle to forgive. Ten minutes into the sermon, I asked everyone to stand, retrieve his or her rock, hold it at arm's length, and grip it tightly in one outstretched hand. After a few moments, I challenged the bemused but cooperative participants to hold their rock tighter, then tighter still. For two minutes I encouraged them to squeeze harder, to intensify the pressure, to clench the rock as if their lives depended on how tightly it was held. I urged them on. With the occasional nervous laugh breaking out, they persisted, intensifying the force applied to the jagged objects they held. Faces reddened. Random grunts erupted. Veins began to bulge.

After two minutes, during which time people grew visibly uncomfortable, I gave a different instruction. "Now, on the count of three, drop the rock." When I reached three, more than 300 rocks hit the floor simultaneously. Even with carpet, the resounding thud was powerful, rich, and deep. Congregants immediately began to smile and rub their aching hands. As they returned to a seated position, I asked, "How did it feel while you were gripping the rock tightly?" They quickly responded with various synonyms for painful. Then I asked, "What one word would you use to describe how it felt to finally let it go?" Their near unanimous answer was, "Relief."

Inviting them to be seated, and without mentioning the rock again, I continued, "To forgive means to let go, to let go of anger, to let go of a need for revenge, to let go of obsessing about how you were hurt, to let go of thinking of yourself as a victim. When you refuse to let go, when you continue to hold on to pain knowing that it's actually hurting you, your spirit cramps and begins to ache. When you maintain a death grip on anger, you are making a choice to waste your precious time and energy, your attention, even your health, on something that is causing you unnecessary pain, but if you finally decide to let go, the thing that you will feel is overwhelming relief."

As the service came to a close, everyone was asked to pick up the rock they had dropped earlier. I challenged the room, "You're the only one who can decide if you are ready to let go. If you are, I invite you to express that symbolically by leaving your rock in one of the offering baskets at the doors as you exit. If you just can't let go yet, please carry your rock home and place it in a prominent place so that you will see it daily and be reminded that God can help you loosen your grip."

About half of the rocks were left in the offering baskets as the service ended; the others were carried home. Even though the service was officially over, it became evident that, for some individuals, the metaphor continued to do its work. Over the next few Sundays, we continued to find the occasional rock left in the offering baskets.

What Is A Metaphor?

At its very best, human language is limited. For instance, someone might describe their child in great detail to you, but you would likely still have difficulty identifying their child in a room filled with other children. If it is difficult to describe one's own child in a way that makes him or her recognizable, how much more difficult is it to do justice describing something as intangible as forgiveness? Just what does forgiveness look like, smell like, or sound like? Has anyone ever touched it or held it? How does one go about explaining something that they have never seen?

Whenever we find ourselves trying to explain something abstract or intangible, whenever we are trying to describe the indescribable, we instinctively reach for metaphor.[1] Since so many of our most common concepts are intangible—love, fear, hope, courage, anxiety, time—metaphor runs rampant through our everyday language. *Love* is a garden that you must tend if you want it to blossom. *Fear* is an immovable obstacle that gets in the way. *Hope* is a crocus breaking through the snow. *Time* is a thief. On average, we use one metaphor for every twenty-five words we speak, or about six metaphors a minute. We intuitively and systematically think in metaphors, verbalizing them as naturally as we do our native language.

Taken literally, a metaphor is always false. Metaphor works its magic by messing with our head. It jolts the brain into action with a statement that is obviously not literally true. If, for example, we hear, "That test was a monster," we immediately know that the test was not, in fact, a threatening creature of terrifying shape and proportion. Rendered uncomfortable by the illogical statement, our brain refuses to rest. Compelled to figure out how the two unlike things are alike, it begins to imaginatively play with possibilities, looking for similarities and differences in its attempt to find a plausible explanation for the odd pairing. In less than a second, it intuitively understands that the test was like a monster because it both intimidated and terrified the one taking it. On the other hand, because it did not hide under their bed or physically threaten them, the test was also unlike a monster in significant ways.

Metaphors are lovely lies in which, by saying one thing while meaning another, a deeper truth is revealed. In employing metaphor, we are taking advantage of old knowledge and using it to create new knowledge as we find ourselves unexpectedly comparing two things that are, at first glance, incomparable. A good metaphor allows us to

---

[1] Metaphor technically includes any comparison made between two seemingly unrelated subjects. They include similes (She runs like a cheetah), synechdoches (At 16, I was extremely proud of my first set of wheels), personification (The trees moaned in the wind), and idioms (The early bird catches the worm). In each case, the words used transcend the literal meaning of what is said.

understand more about an unknown thing because we already know about another thing. Take, for example, a line from the 1977 film, Annie Hall. "A relationship, I think, is like a shark. You know? It has to constantly move forward or it dies. And I think what we got on our hands is a dead shark." The metaphor describes an intangible—a relationship—in terms of something concrete—a cartilaginous fish. Relationships and sharks are not even remotely alike, but in making this unexpected connection between the two, we are skillfully reminded that a stagnant relationship is a dead relationship. Geary observes, "To understand metaphors, literal truth must be quarantined so metaphorical truth can emerge."[2]

There is satisfaction found in discovering the links between the two parts of a metaphor. Geary explains, "Pattern recognition is so basic that the brain's pattern detection modules and its reward circuitry became inextricably linked. Whenever we successfully detect (or map) a pattern—or think we detect a pattern—the neurotransmitters responsible for sensations of pleasure squirt through our brains."[3] With more familiar metaphors, the brain works less.[4] Because we don't have to waste time wondering what it means if we are told that we are 'skating on thin ice,' our brain receives little to no reward. Our brain works harder to figure out an unfamiliar metaphor. The harder our brain works, the more dopamine is released and the more pleasure we experience.

Accordingly, metaphors that are less common are infinitely more powerful. In 2013, the media was suddenly obsessed with the notion of "falling off a fiscal cliff." Forest Gump won our hearts and our attention with "Life is like a box of chocolates. You never know what you're gonna get." Faulkner vividly depicted a man in a state of shock, writing, "He looks like right after the maul hits the steer and it's no longer alive

---

[2] James Geary, *I Is an Other: The Secret Life of Metaphor and How It Shapes the Way We See the World* (New York: HarperCollins, 2011), 53.

[3] Geary, *I Is and Other*, 34-35.

[4] Some metaphors are so commonly used that they are referred to as 'dead metaphors,' having been used so often that they have lost both their original imagery and their power. Examples include 'lend a hand,' 'run for office,' and 'fishing for compliments.'

and don't yet know that it is dead." Comedian Bill Maher jokes, "True Love is like a salesman at Home Depot. It only comes along once or twice in a lifetime, so you've gotta grab it."

According to Harvard Medical School's professor of psychiatry Arnold H. Modell, the unprompted mappings that forge new connections in the mind are exactly what make metaphors potent. They play a dominant role in organizing and categorizing emotional memories. Our strongest memories are frequently triggered by metaphorical representations of an event or person in our past. For me, Camay soap is a metaphor for the home of one of my elementary school friends. Her home always smelled of the powdery, white floral lather. I cannot encounter the fragrance without thinking of her. An avocado green kitchen appliance generates nostalgic thoughts of the 1970's. One taste of cotton candy and I'm at the state fair, surrounded by funnel cakes, Ferris wheels, and funhouses. If I should happen to hear *Good Vibrations* by The Beach Boys, I'm suddenly thrown into a case of confusion because I'm fifteen again, at a school dance, and scared to death that I might not be invited to dance—but even more scared that I will be.

The Power of Metaphor

Metaphorical representations are not restricted to language. Because metaphors are essential to all thinking, they occur in many forms. In the final scene of *Planet of the Apes*, the entire interpretation of the movie drastically changes when the hero comes face-to-face with a larger-than-life visual metaphor that happened to be one of the few surviving icons of a pre-Apocalyptic human society—The Statue of Liberty. In a cartoon, the addition of steam coming from a character's ears is an easily recognizable metaphor for anger. A national flag fluttering in the breeze wordlessly evokes powerful patriotism. A pat on the back when someone needs encouragement says tactilely what may not be said verbally. Other examples of non-verbal metaphors include a football referee pointing their arm toward the defensive team's goal ("First down"), humming the theme music of the TV show *Jeopardy* ("Time is running out"), or violations of realism in a piece of art that indicate there is more than the literal going on. Art, dreams, music, gestures, and institutions all have the ability to serve as powerful metaphors.

Metaphor functions at multiple levels. As previously mentioned, metaphor can fill in a gaping opening in language, conveying meaning when adequate terminology simply does not exist. In addition, the right metaphor can be substituted for entire pages of information. Moreover, the emotion-producing quality of metaphor enhances the memorability of subject matter and makes persuasion and changed behavior more likely. Metaphor can build community because people who share the same stories and metaphors feel connected. Extended metaphor functions superbly as an organizing principle around which to structure a single idea, sermon, or book. Metaphor can be employed to approach a touchy subject in a tactful but effective manner, which is exactly what Nathan did when confronting David about Uriah and Bathsheba.

When the mind is numbed by too many words, a well-chosen metaphor can break through a droning voice and penetrate the defenses. We make a huge mistake when we think the key to teaching is presenting the right information. We may *hear* propositions and data, but we *listen to* and *absorb* metaphor and story.

When people believe the truthfulness of a metaphor, they begin to live into it. Martin Luther King's *I Have a Dream* speech was built entirely on metaphors. In it, racial injustice is a hot and sandy desert filled with dangerous quicksand. Denial of fundamental rights is a defaulted promissory note. The policy of gradualism is a tranquilizing drug. Brotherhood is a symphony. These metaphors shaped the thoughts and actions of a generation. Because metaphor inherently carries attitudes and values, people who are able to impose new metaphors on their culture are able to define what is considered to be true. The right metaphor has the ability to persuade and galvanize people for action like nothing else.

Working in sync with the body to produce meaning, the brain consists of two well-defined hemispheres, both of which collect and sort information to make sense of the world, yet each hemisphere is highly specialized, receiving specific types of information and working toward different agendas. The left hemisphere, the more cognitive side of the brain, processes data and language. It loves facts, logic, and linear organization. The right hemisphere processes images and emotions, recognizes patterns, makes connections, and is creative, intuitive, and impressionistic. Although the hemispheres are separate, they are linked by a wide flat bundle of neural fibers called the corpus callosum that allows them to be in constant communication.

In the early 1970s, at The California Institute of Technology, research was done on neurologically impaired subjects who had their corpus callosum severed in some kind of accident. For this reason, the left and right hemispheres could no longer communicate with each other. Monitored by MRIs, the patients listened to people read. It soon became obvious that when statistics and facts were read, the left side of the subjects' brains kicked into over-drive while the right side remained quiet. When story or metaphor was read, the electrical activity of the left side was somewhat reduced, but it still continued. Meanwhile, the right side showed dramatically increased electrical activity. It was concluded that "The left hemisphere is involved in metaphor comprehension as well as analogical reasoning and the right hemisphere becomes involved due to a kind of 'spillover' when task demands are high."[5]

The implications cannot be ignored. When facts and propositions are presented, only the left side of the brain is firing. When story or metaphor is presented, the entire brain is activated, signaling that something more important is going on. The highly selective brain will attend to the story and metaphor while ignoring everything else. An expert can present all the correct factual information to an audience in a perfectly coherent manner, but unless the right brain is also activated, unless it experiences an emotional connection, those facts are quickly forgotten. On the other hand, if the right brain is activated through metaphor, story, color, and image, it resonates in such a way that the brain grabs on and remembers.

---

[5] Miriam Bassock, Kevin N. Dunbar, and Keith J. Holyoak, "Introduction to the Special Section on the Neural Substrate of Analogical Reasoning and Metaphor Comprehension," *Journal of Experimental Psychology: Learning, Memory, and Cognition* 38, no. 2 (2012): 262. http://0web.ebscohost.com.catalog. georgefox. edu/ehost/ pdfviewer/ pdfviewer? sid=30cb94f9-403b-4a07-9ddf-6ed994bb8dbb%40sessionmgr110&vid=6&hid-107 (accessed January 28, 2013).

Pay Attention to What it Doesn't Say

A metaphor normally focuses on one feature of a concept that has several features. As that one feature comes to the forefront, the other features remain out of focus. Remember the earlier example, "That test was a monster"? Consciously, we only think about the similarities between the test and the monster, not the differences—yet unconsciously the mappings our brain makes are never without significant differences. Geary observes, "The paradox of metaphor is that it tells us so much about a person, place, or thing by telling us what that person, place, or thing is not," but because we seldom deliberately think about the mappings, even though the differences remain, they remain under the mind's radar. [6]

As a result, choosing the wrong metaphor can be disastrous. Consider the common metaphorical association between *argument* and *war*. They link up easily because we have come to think of both as a kind of conflict. In both we want to *win the battle*. We *attack the weaknesses* of our adversary. We *shoot down* illogical points. We want to *demolish* our foe. What if there was a way to reprogram the mind to associate *argument* with *dance,* both of which are types of social engagements? Perhaps our arguments would become less hostile and more graceful. Like a dance, an argument could be thought of as an *interaction* between two parties characterized by a *natural rhythm of give-and-take,* a *shared encounter* that could ultimately result in the two parties moving closer together. Perhaps we could even argue in a more playful spirit. The metaphor really does matter.

The more difficult and abstract a concept is to explain, the more metaphors will be needed to describe it. Love, for instance, is not only spoken of as if it were a physical force that can sweep us off our feet, it is also an object or destination for which we search. Love is an illness (He's lovesick), a mental disorder (I'm crazy in love), a plant (He cultivated her love), and a game (He's toying with her affections). Likewise, life can be described metaphorically as a journey, a game, a possession, a story, or a day. A concept as unfathomable as God cries out for numerous metaphors: father, mother, light, craftsperson, poet,

---

[6] Geary, *I Is an Other,* 12.

physician, judge, king, lover, gardener, rock, potter, and wisdom (to name but a few). Each metaphor reveals one aspect of who God is. None will reveal God in his entirety.

Embodied Metaphor

Metaphorical mappings are not just a mental thing. "Much recent research and theory points to how metaphor relies on interactions between the auditory, visual, kinesthetic areas of the brain and the entire human body in the physical-cultural world more generally."[7] Even though our mind technically knows the difference between what is real and what is metaphorical, our body reacts to reality and metaphor the same way. If someone calls us "trash," we momentarily respond to the phrase as if it were reality. For a microsecond, we feel 'trashy'—dirty, unclean, possibly disposable. It is as if the metaphor triggers a momentary short circuit in our mind that causes thought to briefly jump the track from operating in the left hemisphere to the right hemisphere.

Good metaphor always activates our senses. If we hear, "The dragonflies zoomed across the glittering pond like miniature biplanes," both our visual and auditory centers are drafted to process the sentence. In hearing someone comment on the stale cardboard taste of pre-packaged communion wafers, the areas of the brain that process taste, touch, sight, hearing, and smell are activated. Metaphors describing motion activate the motor cortex. Like good stories, the best metaphors trick our brain into reality responses. Because the entire body is recruited to interpret a metaphor, any new insight travels across multiple neural pathways, making it more memorable.

All metaphors are embodied, meaning they are grounded in real-life experience. To make connections between two things, a person has to have significant direct experience with at least one of those things. For example, a person from Suriname who has never watched American TV could not possibly understand the sentence, "Your life has more drama than Maury Povich!" Similarly, a passing metaphorical reference

---

[7] Raymond W. Gibbs Jr., *The Cambridge Handbook of Metaphor and Thought*, ed. Raymond W. Gibbs Jr. (Cambridge University Press: New York, 2008), 8.

to the genius of Michelangelo, Donatello, Rafael, and Leonardo made to a group of third graders would be more likely to jumpstart a series of associations having nothing to do with Renaissance artists and everything to do with *Heroes in a Half-Shell.*

Metaphors in Church

The church has moved too far to the left—at least too far to the left-brain. We have confused a fixation on information with a foundation for transformation. We have grown convinced that communicating propositions is the same as offering spiritual nutrition. Hitting a congregation with everything we know may make us feel good about ourselves, but it does little to help the listeners embrace transformation. "Listeners, already drowning in a tidal wave of information, simply can't respond to another similar sounding bucketful thrown in their faces," argues Anne Miller.[8]

For those who preach Jesus Christ, to be satisfied with merely presenting cold, hard facts or even flowery propositions is a dereliction of duty. When presenting the Good News, it is our duty to do so in ways that truly communicate the lengths God goes to in order to demonstrate his love for us. Metaphor and story communicate it best, resonating in deep ways, penetrating numbed mental matter while forcing others to 'see' what we mean by experiencing it viscerally. When you move from using propositions to using metaphor, you are allowing your listeners to see what you mean in ways that have staying power, ways that are vivid, attention grabbing, and emotional. When the hearers are both physically and emotionally shaken, the listeners don't just remember—they are moved to action.

Therefore, metaphor is a critical tool for any teacher or preacher. It mediates experiential knowledge and underpins the faith. It shifts Scripture from the realm of theology to the realm of autobiography. Our task is to create appropriate metaphors for teaching a concept and then

---

[8] Anne Miller, *Metaphorically Selling: How to Use the Magic of Metaphors to Sell, Persuade, & Explain Anything to Anyone* (New York: Chiron Associates Inc, 2004), 9.

step back—allowing the listener to unconsciously interact with them in a reflexive search for similarities. Their meaning-making brains are eagerly waiting to do the interpretive work.

There's a good chance that making up metaphors does not come naturally to you. That can change. As you intentionally expose yourself to more metaphors, and as you deliberately try to create them, your ability improves—much as your ability to speak a foreign language would improve the more you practiced it. Yes, it will take effort on your part to grow more fluent in the language of metaphor, but knowing that one tiny phrase might be the clap of thunder that awakes a sleeping giant makes it well worth your time to practice, practice, practice.

Those who preach should continuously be scanning the horizon for appropriate metaphors to be used in sharing the Gospel. As we creatively use metaphor, God is allowing us to share in his creativity. We become image-makers for God as we imagine God in new and meaningful ways, ways that allow others to envision him afresh as well. We have the high and holy privilege of naming options that others can use to reflect on the Eternal One. Jesus did just this as he worked to change and supplement some of the metaphors used to describe God in his day. Instead of speaking of God as lawmaker and judge, he introduced a God who is tender shepherd, loving father, mother hen, bread that nourishes, and wine that brings joy.

There is no way to talk about God without resorting to metaphor, but because every metaphor is limited, it is necessary to introduce our congregations to multiple metaphors—each of which will give a small glimpse of his character. Truth has many levels. Settling for only one metaphor, or even a few with which we especially identify, limits insight into who God is. For instance, one metaphorical image of God in Scripture is conquering warrior. There is truth to be found in that metaphor, but if that image is not fused to other images, the single metaphor can lead us to believe in a militaristic, merciless God. Without the mediating force of other metaphors, one metaphor will create a false idol.

Metaphors should not be chosen lightly. The metaphors you employ are brimming over with behavioral implications. They affect what you believe, how you pray, and how you relate to others. As you work to create appropriate metaphors, ask the following questions: (1) In one word or phrase, what is the main concept that I want to teach? (2) Is there something to which that concept can be compared that might give my hearers a new lens with which to view God? If you are drawing a blank, try doing an image search on the concept. Scrolling through artist renditions of that image can jumpstart your right brain. (3) Does my audience have some familiarity with the thing with which I am comparing God, Jesus, justice, compassion, etc.? (4) When taken literally, is the comparison false? If it is true, it is not a metaphor. (5) Does this comparison distort the truth or present a false impression? (6) Do I use a variety of metaphors when talking about God, or do I repeatedly return to the same one? (7) Does the language I use voicing the metaphor engage the senses? (8) Is there a physical representation that would be appropriate to use as a prop or project onto the big screen?

The best preachers and teachers are all metaphor collectors who build a reserve to pull from as needed. They keep their eyes open and their ears alert, all the while knowing that they are surrounded by expressions of eternal truth. It has been said that truth is a competition between metaphors. Advertising and media are both strong contenders in the contest, but so far, the church has not even begun to run the race. She may have bought a new pair of running shoes. She may have done a few stretches to warm up, but she has yet to run the metaphorical race set before her.

Chapter 11

REMEMBERING AS A TEAM

In the neighborhood where I grew up, it was expected that little girls would learn to play the piano whether they wanted to do or not. For their mothers, it was a matter of pride. They each anticipated the day when their daughter would become skilled enough to show off her keyboard prowess during a worship service by playing during the offertory. My own mother shared that dream, hoping that I would take my place among the gifted pianists in our congregation.

Although I had no desire to play, Mama bought a piano and worked extra hours to pay for lessons. To be honest, it was very difficult for me to be grateful for something I did not particularly want—especially when there was something else I wanted very much. I wanted to take art lessons. I would have gladly invested my heart and soul in studying contour drawing, learning to mix colors, preparing canvases, and mastering palette knives.

Instead, from age seven to ten—with no natural ability whatsoever—I begrudgingly slogged through finger exercises, learned to read notes, and attempted to master rhythm. It was hopeless. No matter how hard I tried, my left hand simply refused to cooperate with my right. I could learn to play the correct notes with either hand, but when I tried to put them together, I mangled the music. Dreading the weekly lesson, I 'forgot' to walk to the home of my teacher after school. I found excuses to skip practicing, no longer caring if I received a once coveted gold star sticker after playing a piece for my teacher.

Finally, in exasperation, she called my mother and uttered words that came as a great relief to me even as they wounded my mother. "Mrs.

Champion, can Paula please quit taking lessons? She's wasting my time and your money."

My mother grieved. Yes, her pride was hurting, but even more importantly, she was convinced that I would never have a place of service in our church where, because I was female, service during worship was restricted to making music. She had heard me sing, so she viewed the piano as my only hope. When I proved a total failure in both areas, she was convinced the door to service had been slammed in my face.

In some ways she was correct. Our church, a microcosm of church culture in the Deep South at the time, placed great value on speaking and musical talent. Males who could speak coherently and confidently were encouraged, even pushed, to serve as preachers. Musical ability, on the other hand, was valued in both sexes. Even a female could proclaim the gospel if she did it set to music. Technically, we were taught that all Christians were gifted to serve. In reality, the majority of us quietly sat on the sidelines while our star speakers and musicians actually played the game. There seemed to be no place of service for the poet, the painter, the dancer, the bookworm, the writer, the storyteller, the engineer, the song writer, the decorator, the brainiac, or the actor among us.

A different, but parallel attitude existed in our youth group. It celebrated jocks, cheerleaders, and student council members. They were put on the Youth Council, recruited to help out at community events, and praised for being great examples of Christian involvement. I once heard a youth director say, "If you really want to grow a youth group, go after the popular kids first. If you can get them involved, everyone else will follow along." Once again, the artsy, brainy, and more introverted kids were virtually invisible. It wasn't that they weren't willing to put their talents to work in the church. It was that they were never invited to do so. No one imagined they had anything worthwhile to offer.

Toward a More Complete Body

Paul compares the church to a body with different parts designed to carry out different purposes. In 1 Corinthians 12:17, he asks, "If the whole body were an eye, where would the sense of hearing be? If the whole body were an ear, where would the sense of smell be?" He understood that the church needs every part functioning if she is to be healthy. Most Christians give lip service to that fact. Unfortunately, the same Christians can be guilty of valuing some gifts above others to the point that they act as if some people are more desirable than others. Perhaps that is one reason the church is struggling so today.

But what if... What if we intentionally searched out and put to work the gift of every member? What if we let the geeks and nerds know that they are as highly valued as the preachers and musicians? What if we set the artist and the poet free to serve publically? What if we told the movie aficionado that the church needed their help planning worship? What if we treasured the offering of a librarian as much as that of a musician?

That's exactly what we will have to do if we are to effectively use brain-based teaching methods. Designing brain-based worship experiences is labor-intensive, both physically and mentally. Few individuals have the time or the talents to implement brain-based design without the help of a team of creative thinkers. Because one person cannot do it alone, a worship-design team is an indispensable tool.

The ideal team would be composed of all individuals involved leading worship. It would also include several decidedly creative individuals who have the gift of imagination. Finally, you would need a couple of left-brained, highly organized, practical people who can evaluate the feasibility of off-the-wall ideas and assist in implementing the enthusiastic imaginings of artists. So how does one go about finding such a team?

Developing a Team

Begin by getting to know your people. Talk to them. Listen to them. Ask them about their interests and hobbies. Ask what activities can totally absorb their time and attention. Ask them about the interests and hobbies of their family members. Visit their homes. Pay attention while there. Good observation will indicate who is a meticulous decorator, who has original art on the walls, who sews, who has photos of dance recitals, who is engaged with a community theater, and who does photography.

In addition, ask. When I created a simple survey that listed about twenty-five hobbies and interests, we discovered forty-four people in our congregation who were involved in the arts in one way or another. Through it, we discovered human resources we did not know we had and people who, restless and unused, were excited about being given an opportunity to contribute something of themselves to our worship services.

Finally, invite. Using the pulpit and church publications, let the your congregation know that you are looking for a group of creative, committed, hard-working people to form a worship planning team. Emphasize that, although they are welcome, you are not necessarily looking for professionals. You are looking for people with the gift of imagination—idea people, artsy people, creative people, craftsmen, people with technical skills, movie-buffs, decorators, and videographers. You are looking for dreamers, for co-creators. You are also looking for people who have experience working with learning centers and have a solid foundation of good, basic teaching methods used to communicate core content, so school teachers would be a great addition to the team.

Be honest with your people. Tell them that serving will require a deep commitment to making weekly worship happen, and that most of the work will be behind the scenes so they may never be recognized for what they do. Let them know the worship planning team is an open team. People can join and leave as desired, so it's OK just to come check it out and see if they are interested before committing to it. It's OK to come and work through a sermon series and see how they like it. Finally, tell them that the only qualifications they need to serve on the worship planning team are a strong desire to assist others connect to God, a willingness to take ownership of parts of the worship service, and a readiness to go the extra mile in preparing for worship. Announce a time and place for a team formation meeting for those who are interested in learning more.

At this point, you are probably thinking two things. First, you may be thinking that it is useless to extend such an invitation because there are no artistic people in your church, but there are—perhaps not professionals, but large numbers of people who do not make their living as professional artists still enjoy creating paintings and drawings for their own homes. Others write songs or poetry, do photography, and edit videos for their personal enjoyment. A few have an innate ability to arrange the elements of a room (or a stage) in such a way that they capture and focus attention. Just because these are not things you will hear them talk about publically does not mean they aren't doing them.

Second, you are probably thinking that with an open invitation you will have no control over who shows up. Believe it or not, that's a good thing. God has a habit of putting his Holy Spirit to work in the most unlikely candidates. It is impossible for human eyes to see the potential for God-possibilities in others. God tends to gravitate to dubious, improbable, even eccentric sorts. I seriously doubt that the austere-dressing, bug-eating John the Baptist, the Roman collaborator and Jewish traitor Matthew, the working girl Rahab, the prophetess Huldah, or the young whippersnapper Timothy would have ever been chosen as a candidate for a leadership position in their local house of worship. I doubt anyone ever looked at scrawny David as he picked burrs from his sheep's wool and thought, "Wow! That boy is going to be the greatest writer of poetry and song to ever live!" Yet, God used each of them in a different way to reveal who he is. The biggest mistake you can make is to try to limit who God can use. That is the sure-fire formula for failure. If however you accept those who show up because they want to be there for no other reason than to make worship more worshipful, you are accepting them as a gift from God through whom his Spirit can work. And yes, for control freaks, this can be a big leap of faith.

Know that some who show up may not be your typical church people. The more creative a person is, the more eccentric they may appear on the surface, and the more sensitive they may be emotionally. There's a reason that musicians are considered high-strung and artists are deemed emotional; they usually are more in touch with their emotions. Generally, they are more sensitive to the environment around them, to the moods of others, to nuances of meaning, and to sensory details. They tend to express emotions with more ease than their left-brained counterparts. Many creative personalities consider this hypersensitivity to be a burden. You can help them see it as a divine gift that they can offer back to God. Their sensitivity is what will allow them to create emotional depth that will spur transformation in participants.

Chances are, you will not find all your team members at once. Don't be afraid to start small. After the initial group forms, continue to look for individuals who might be an asset to the team. Urge team members to do the same. Talent attracts talent. If someone paints, they will almost surely know others who paint. If someone is a computer whizz, they will know others who share their interest. Encourage the team to make use of their connections and invite other creatives to join you. Each person who shows up will add their own twist to the ideas generated and to the final product. Don't be afraid to use sporadic attenders if they volunteer to help. I have seen them move toward much deeper levels of commitment while serving on the team.

But what if you have too many people show up? What if you end up with a group of thirty? How do thirty people plan worship together? They don't. If you have more than you need for a worship planning team, form two teams, even three. In this ideal situation, the teams can take turns planning sermon series. This will help prevent burnout and keep services fresh.

The Initial Meeting

At the first meeting of interested parties, inform everyone that your desire is to do a better job communicating the Gospel. Explain that they are there to dream about how that might happen. Talk briefly about your dreams for worship and for the team—how you think worship can improve, where you see it going in the future, why you think a worship planning team can lead the congregation to more frequent encounters with God, and how you envision the team functioning.

When you are through, invite those present to dream out loud. What parts of the worship service do they find tedious? What could make worship more meaningful? Are there portions they do not understand—perhaps terminology or why something is done the same way every week? Does anything make them uncomfortable? What? Why? Is there any part to which they look forward? How would they imagine a perfect service to look, sound, and feel?

Ask what they think they can personally contribute to the process. Do they see themselves as idea people, artists, seamstresses, videographers, directors and coordinators of what everyone else is doing, or what? Do they have more than one area of interest? Given a choice in how they can serve, team members will be more motivated to come through with quality contributions. Give them all the time they need to discuss their opinions and ideas. Take notes.

Afterwards, announce that the team will meet again in two weeks. Ask those who are still interested in serving on the team to leave their email addresses. Explain that you will be sending them a synopsis of an upcoming series in the next twenty-four hours. This will include a listing of each week's Scripture passage and a one-sentence description of the accompanying sermon.

For example, if you are preaching a series on the Beatitudes, the week you get to Matthew 5:5 (*Blessed are the meek, for they will inherit the earth.*), a one sentence summary for your worship team to work with might read, "Meekness is strength under control." This sentence is the cornerstone upon which everything else will be built. Include the fact that you will be telling the story of the Syrophoenician Woman from Mark 7:25–30 as an example of meekness.

Request that they read through the information they receive, pray about it, and begin to imagine ways to creatively communicate each week's message. Encourage them to think in terms of appropriate metaphors, film clips, Bible stories, stories of individuals in the church, songs, supplemental activities, images, and stage and altar decorations. Acquaint them with websites such as www.sermonspice.com, www.worshiphousemedia.com, www.worshipfilms.com, and www.sermoncentral.com. Tell them that you want them to be ready to talk about possibilities for creatively communicating the series at the next meeting. Finally, turn them lose to imagine possibilities on their own.

The Practical Process

Assuming that every service is planned around a scriptural story, the person preaching has the task of choosing the passage, the theme, the story to be told, and the message to be conveyed. Normally, about six weeks before a series begins, the team should have the above-mentioned sermon series summation in hand. Long before the actual planning meeting occurs, everyone involved needs to have a solid grasp of the messages to be delivered. Without this, design will go nowhere fast. The worship-planning meeting is not the time to figure out where a sermon series is going. It is instead the time to flesh it out.

Give the team two weeks to mull over the information they have received, encouraging them to read through the Scripture passages daily. This time period allows time for the Holy Spirit to work as ideas begin to percolate and mature. Beginning the process this far in advance pays off with better, more effective ideas for communicating the message of Scripture.

The person leading the worship planning meeting will have the responsibility of unlocking the creative potential of team members and directing their energy. To do this, he or she will have to create a high level of trust and respect within the team. Members should be encouraged to be honest but tactful as they discuss each other's ideas. They should expect opinions to differ and understand that no one individual will ever have all the best plans. If the process is working as it should, every member of the team will sometimes offer an off-the-wall idea that would never work. Far-fetched suggestions should not only be expected, they should be celebrated. Nothing assists a brainstorming session like the freedom to imagine, and nothing spurs a good imagination like bouncing improbable ideas off people you trust. The most important aspect of planning is never the talent of individual team members anyway. The real power is in the ideas that a focused team can generate and carry out together.

Insist that nothing be critiqued while brainstorming. If someone begins to criticize an idea, remind everyone that the brainstorming time is a time to play with ideas, a time to have fun. No idea should be regarded as too outlandish. When proposals can flow freely, bizarre ideas often generate more practical ones. Write each suggestion down on a large white board (or whatever you have available that is large enough for everyone to see).

Before the brainstorming portion of the meeting ever begins, be honest with your team about what resources are available—especially budget-wise. Most churches realistically have limited financial resources, so budget must constantly be kept in mind while planning. No matter how great an idea may be, if it cannot be practically implemented it is useless. Thankfully, many of the best activities require little to no budget.

Keep in mind that the worship planning-team is producing an artisanal expression of worship for their congregation by using their unique gifts and interest to communicate the Gospel message. Original, user-generated worship services will speak mega-decibels louder than services 'copied' from other churches—no matter how well it worked elsewhere. Customize for your community by building each service from scratch. As you do, you will discover that the result is always more than the sum of its parts. Something beautiful happens as the team puts effort into listening to and communicating the word of God week after week.

Designing a Series

The initial planning meeting for a series will be long, possibly 3 hours. If the team has done their homework, by the end of the time period the entire series will be mapped out. During the series itself, weekly tweaks and fine adjustments can be made via a chat room. Choose a time when members will to be able to stay for the entire time—a Saturday morning, a Sunday afternoon, whatever works best for them.

Begin the process by choosing a metaphor for the entire series. The metaphor chosen for the series will tie all the services together.[1] Perhaps one of the Scripture passages already contains a usable metaphor. If not, what is the congregation familiar with that might convey the theme of this series? Has anyone discovered any material on one of the websites that could be used? What about a piece of art or scene from a movie or TV show? Do not hesitate to throw your own ideas out to the group for evaluation during brainstorming. Especially during the first few planning sessions, they may need assistance understanding the concept of choosing a metaphor to capture the essence of a series.

---

[1] Appendix A offers an example of a sermon series planned this way. You may want to refer to it as you continue to read.

Once the metaphor for the series is in place, continue to build on that metaphor as you plan the weekly services. Talk briefly about how each week's message will relate to the metaphor. Revisit the Scripture and the sermon in a sentence for each week. Begin the brainstorming process all over again for each week of the series, asking those present to suggest ideas about how the message can best be communicated. Encourage recommendations for film clips, sensory stimulation, hands-on activities, illustrations, images, metaphors, and rituals. Remember to include ways to reflect upon the sermon and activities, keeping in mind that reflection evokes the emotions that move experiential knowledge to long-term memory. Keep a record of all ideas in front of everyone.

After allowing time for sufficient brainstorming, revisit the ideas. Talk through them, narrowing them down by continually referring each back to the sermon in a sentence. If the idea or activity is not communicating the needed message, no matter how good it may be, it only gets in the way of actual learning. Determine which options will be the most suitable ones for communicating the message. Which suggestions convey the theme or Scripture best? What proposals are directly related to the theme metaphor? Which ones are doable in your setting? What images would work with the sermon in a sentence? What physical representations could be used? What activities can be used to engage the senses? What is your team capable of doing with quality?

This last question is particularly important. It is always better to do less and do it very well than to do several things halfway. This is especially true when you are first beginning to include new elements in a service. When adding new components to existing worship services, it is usually better to go slowly. This allows the new to become 'normalized' and thus less threatening.

The Design Process

As options are narrowed down to the most workable, effective ones, decisions must be made about design. It does no good to introduce choices, sensory stimulation, or emotional elements into a teaching situation without doing the necessary design work needed to make it productive. In designing a service, you are putting the creative content into some kind of workable order, deciding how to assemble a collage of learning opportunities, each of which will reinforce the same content, eventually resulting in thick layers of meaning that will cling to the minds and hearts of worshippers.

In the past, we have called this an *Order of Worship,* and it was linear and predictable. With the sermon considered the high point of the service, you started *here* and ended *there* with no diverging paths in between. That *Order of Worship* will not be as predictable when using brain-based methodology.[2] The fact that choices are offered to worshippers means that not everyone will be doing the same thing at the same moment. Some may choose to arrive early and take advantage of activities at the stations. Others may stay late to do the same. During the service itself, considerable time will be allotted to utilize stations, to receive communion, to pray with others, or to contribute to a discussion.

Gunter Kress, professor of semiotics and education at the University of London, argues that because we are presently undergoing a shift from a linear, mono-modal style of learning and teaching to a multimodal style in which the teacher organizes or assembles multiple ways to access information and material, the way the elements are put together is key.[3] No matter how good the ideas are, if thought is not put into how to make all elements flow together in such a way as to give rise to one central truth, the participants will benefit little. Even in the most creative atmosphere, chaos should never reign.

It may help to think of the design process as the act of orchestrating the service. In an orchestra, a group of highly competent musicians come together to make music, but they don't begin to play without meticulous planning. Otherwise, they will produce a cacophony of unrelated sounds. The conductor must make decisions about the works to be performed, the sequence of the music, who plays what and when, and the tempo of the performance. He or she works to shape the sound of the performers, execute clear plans and preparations, and relay information to the performers.

---

[2] See Appendix 2 for an example of the design/order of worship for one service..
[3] Gunther R. Kress, *Multimodality: A Social Semiotic Approach to Contemporary Communication* (London: Routledge, 2010), 139.

Similarly, worship designers develop the details of the service, making decisions about the sequence of components, the mood, and the tempo and pace of all the different elements. They work to unify and coordinate the activities of many people in order to accomplish something greater than the effort of any one individual. Especially important is the assigning of responsibilities for each element of the service. Before the planning meeting ends, make sure someone has accepted responsibility for constructing every station, assigning every reading, securing needed props, and arranging the stage, altar, or entryway. This is where you left-brained organizers shine. We had one member who came to our design meetings and never said a word, but two or three days later he would send us a coded chart for each service that included who was doing what, when they were doing it, and what resources were needed.

Well-crafted design enables the learner to couple one sensory idea or activity with a different sensory idea or activity—a written text with an image, a soundtrack with a fragrance, an emotion with a color or taste. No matter how appropriate any one sensory activity might be, it must interact with other modes, each providing one lens to a complex reality. Because the learner must want to participate, the design needs to be welcoming and non-threatening. Make sure each supplemental activity offers clear, well-thought-out oral or written instructions explaining how each activity works, what is expected from those who join in, and how participants can get the most out of it. Doing this well gives everyone a level playing field on which to learn. When participants are enabled to interact bodily in the worship experience, they create new meaning for themselves—not theoretical meaning but personal meaning.

According to interactive design specialist Edwin Schlossberg, "To assist the interactive experiences, to complement this more intuitive strategy of learning, there needs to be access to learning that is more traditional in its approach and more goal-oriented."[4] Above all, the designer must remember that language—be it written or spoken—is always the primary mode for conveying knowledge. Schlossberg contends, "It would be as confusing to suggest that all learning could take place experientially and interactively as it used to be to suggest

---

[4] Edwin Schlossberg, *Interactive Excellence: Defining and Developing New Standards for the Twenty-First Century* (New York: Ballantine Books, 1998), 61.

that all learning should be presented in a goal-oriented style. It is the combination of the two styles, presented with the appropriate content in each, that will create the best climate for learning."[5] Consequently, the spoken word will never loose its power. It always has been and always will remain the primary teaching tool God uses. It becomes even more powerful when augmented by appropriate images, activities, stories, and metaphors.

Because elements of brain-based teaching can be used in any size group, they can be implemented in a church of twenty-five or a church of five hundred. Of course, adjustments must be made to accommodate different size groups. In a smaller church, a three or four person team may be large enough to instigate and execute weekly activities. A larger church will need a full team of designers (or even better, two teams) and duplicates of each station to accommodate more participants.

Some churches are now employing a staff member whose primary job is to lead the design team. Pastor Mark Pierson, a pioneer in this area, has developed the concept of *worship curator* based on that of a museum curator—the person who "acquires, cares for, develops, displays, and interprets a collection of artifacts of art in order to inform, educate, and entertain the public."[6] A worship curator paves the way for worship by collecting, developing, and preparing multiple opportunities for participation during worship. Pierson argues, "Lasting change usually comes from entering into liminal moments that are occupied by God. . . . In worship, liminal moments are more likely to arise from questions than they are from statements. . . . It isn't possible to create liminal experiences, only to provide situations and settings in which they may occur."[7] Good design does not guarantee that people will interact with God during worship; it does, however, set the stage to make life-changing encounters more likely to happen. Executed well, brain-based services can leave impressions that are unforgettable, motivating more life-change than logical, left-brain lectures ever could.

---

[5] Schlossberg, *Interactive Excellence,* 73.

[6] Mark Pierson, *The Art of Curating Worship: Reshaping the Role of Worship Leader* (Minneapolis, MN: Sparkhouse Press, 2010), 31.

[7] Ibid., 114.

Memorandum: A Conclusion

Church potluck dinner was a Wednesday night staple. I always looked forward to sampling the specialties of the first-class country cooks in our community. The crowded tables in the dining hall would display a veritable rainbow of Southern delicacies—buttery yellow squash, intensely acidic red tomatoes, colored butterbeans, deep green collards, dark olive-green beans, pale yellow-green limas, golden fried green tomatoes or okra, magenta beets, fluffy white potatoes, chestnut colored pintos, creamy yellow corn, peppery orange rutabaga, and cool slices of pink watermelon and sunset yellow cantaloupes.

But week after week, the table everyone checked out first was the dessert table. Would Lillie Mae bring a buttery pound cake or a platter of her thick chocolate chip cookies? Would Velma bake the coconut pies she was known for or go for her more tart lemon meringue? Would Doll remember how much everyone loved her rich dark chocolate pies? With Mardi Gras approaching, would Sidney bring his traditional New Orleans pralines? No matter what was on the table, we knew it would be homemade, and we knew nothing would be left by the end of the meal, until . . .

One week, the one-in-ten-thousand happened. Every person who came, every single person, brought a dessert. Supper consisted of forty-something different manifestations of sugar, each more tempting than the one before it. At first, we all joked that it was a dream come true. With plates piled high, we dug in with gusto.

It did not take long for us to slow down. It turned out that overloading on sugar was not as satisfying as we had dreamed. Overindulging was temporarily filling, but in the long run, our bodies felt uncomfortable, bloated, and sluggish. No one went back for seconds that evening; some didn't finish their first plate—and there were leftovers, lots of leftovers. We may not have understood all the chemical processes taking place inside our bodies at the time, but what we did understand was that we had just had too much of a good thing.

What is true for food is true for nearly every thing that we humans enjoy or value. We have a tendency to go to extremes. Some will build their lives around exercise, choosing to work out rather than spend time with family or relax. Cleaning is a necessary part of life, but compulsive cleaning crosses a line into unhealthy behavior. Excessive reading can interfere with getting important chores done. Even prayer can be carried too far if it is used as an excuse not to do something about that for which one is praying.

For several centuries, the church has made the mistake of taking their love of highly structured, left-brain worship to the extreme. We have overindulged the brain, believing that the best worship services dished-out huge helpings of intellectual information. Convinced that a theoretical grasp of who God is and what he desires was enough, we have sometimes scoffed at the emotionalism of charismatics while priding ourselves on our own logic. With the best of intentions, we have been guilty of generously feeding the brain while unintentionally starving the spirit and body.

Designing effective, God-honoring worship services will not however mean that we check-in our brains at the church-house door. There will always be a need for doing the work of interpreting ancient Scripture for modern audiences, for wrestling with what it 'meant' so we can proclaim what it 'means.' Experience alone is never enough. Through experience, we may be able to discern God's living acts of concern for us and his direction in specific situations, but experience must be balanced with instruction. God is who God has revealed himself to be, not who we fantasize him to be. He invites us to get to know him by loving him with our mind. This signifies that there is an intellectual side to faith we neglect at our own peril. We can only come to know the God of Abraham, Isaac, and Jacob, the God who revealed himself through Jesus, as we read and study Scripture, as we do the hard work of studying the context in which it was written, and as we intentionally expose ourselves to the oldest teachings and traditions of the church. To do otherwise is to diminish the importance of God's self-revelation.

Yes, we have carried intellectual, knowledge-based worship too far. On the other hand, proponents of intellectual, knowledge-based worship are not the only ones who can present one-dimensional, shallow worship experiences. Supporters of embodied knowledge can also go overboard. They can slip into the polarity of dualism just as easily as those who value the mind over the body. In their enthusiasm to engage the emotions and the body, they can neglect the mind. As the slogan of The United Negro College Fund reminds us, "A mind is a terrible thing to waste."

If we are to use the best possible teaching methods, we must ". . . move away from the dualistic structures of body and mind and understand learning as a process that embodies all kinds of moments in its emergence."[1] In other words, we must we return to the past—to ancient Judaism's view of humanity. The Jewish people viewed the body as a God-given sacred tool that allows us to do God's work in the world and to discern his presence and action. The body is a gift to be respected, protected, enjoyed, and cared for. It is holy.

In contrast, the rest of the ancient world was embracing Greek philosophy, relegating the physical world, including the human body, to the category of *evil*. Viewed as the cause of all our problems, the physical body was viewed as a disposable container to be disdained and restrained during life and escaped at death. If that sounds familiar, it is because it is still a prevalent belief. The church in which I was raised frequently proclaimed or implied that the world was evil and that our bodies were nothing more than sources of temptation that would be discarded when we were perfected in God's presence. Without knowing it, I was in a Gnostic evangelical church.

The same church that vilified my human body ironically taught me that God himself honored the human body in the incarnation of Jesus Christ. The word *incarnate* comes from combining the Latin prefix

---

[1] Richard Jordi, "Reframing the Concept of Reflection," *Adult Education Quarterly* 61, no. 2 (2011): 7. http://aeq.sagepub.com/content/61/2/181.abstract (accessed April 10, 2012).

in (made) with the word *caro (flesh or meat)*. You may have used the Latin word in a different sense: *chili con carne*. Chili *con carne* is chili with meat in the beans. Jesus *incarnate* is God with meat on his bones. After Jesus' resurrection, he proved that he still had meat on his bones when he invited Thomas to touch him. He was a whole being—body, mind, and spirit.

Like Jesus, each person is a unity, a composite of body, mind, and spirit. Unfortunately, we have come to mistakenly believe Greek philosophy more than we believe God's self-revelation. Respected Jewish theologian Abraham Heschel points out, "The categories within which philosophical reflection about religion has been operating are derived from Athens rather than from Jerusalem."[2] He goes on to write, "The Greeks learned in order to comprehend. The Hebrews learned in order to revere. The modern man learns in order to use."[3]

What an apt description of our consumer-oriented, modern church culture. We can be guilty of worshipping God in order to use Him—answered prayers, spiritual power, financial stability, or health. In doing so, we are attempting to manipulate God. If instead we worship God in order to know him better and revere him more, especially when he doesn't come through with our desires, we are worshipping God in spirit and in truth.

If the church of the 21st century is to offer worship that is pleasing to God, she must do so by coming at worship from a different angle than she presently does, understanding that God is only partially known in abstract, academic ways. We must end our obstinate attempt to turn the Bible into a systemized textbook and approach it like the family storybook that it is. We must loosen our control on what God is saying, forgoing propositions for scriptural stories while trusting the Holy Spirit to speak through his Word to those who listen. We must set our people free to use their creative gifts, while we work to create a safe place to ask questions and to admit that sometimes we don't have answers. We must reject the temptation to be the all-knowing sage on the stage as we take on the less visible role of a guide on the side, presenting our people

---

[2] Abraham Joshua Heschel, *Noonday*, vol. N526, *God in Search of Man: a Philosophy of Judaism* (New York: Farrar, Straus and Giroux, 1976, 1955), 25.

[3] Ibid., 34.

with options for meeting with a God over which we admittedly have no control. Our goal in designing worship must be decidedly more holistic, taking into account that because humans are a unity of body, mind, and spirit, all must be addressed and invited to join in an encounter with the living God. As we assist others in rediscovering the intimate connection between body, mind, and spirit, we will find our churches moving beyond an intellectual dalliance with a theoretical god and into the beauty of a full-bodied, passionate, divine romance that leaves no room for competing affections.

Appendix 1

EXAMPLE OF ADVENT WORSHIP SERIES

SERIES METAPHOR: EXPECTING A BABY

This series is built around the experience of expecting a baby. Each week details the choices and adjustments new parents (including Mary and Joseph) find themselves making when a new life enters their family. Those choices and adjustments are then related to similar choices and adjustments that accompany the new life Jesus offers.

SERIES THEME: WE'RE EXPECTING

SERMONS:

Week 1- We're Expecting the Unexpected	Matthew 1:18–21
Week 2- We're Expecting to Take Detours	Luke 2:1–7
Week 3- We're Expecting New Life	Luke 2: 8–20
Week 4- We're Expecting Others To Celebrate With Us	Mathew 2:1–11
Week 5- We're Expecting A Change In Priorities	Matthew 2:1–12

VISUALS FOR THE THEME

- Use the Advent colors royal blue and pink to decorate the church. These colors correlate well with the pink and blue of baby shower decorations. Consider using pink and blue ribbons and ornaments with greenery to create wreaths for the front door, to surround hurricane candles in the windows, and as garland across the stage.
- *Alter:* Cover the altar with pink and blue cloths. Top it with a large white cross. Construct candleholders for the altar by using the multicolored rings from a stacking-toy. Glue rings together. Slice off 1.5 inches of center stacking pole. Place rings on pole. Insert candle in top. Add a few other baby related items around the cross to enhance the visual impact (piggy bank, teddy bear, stack of story books, etc.).
- *Lobby/Narthex:* Place a nine-foot tall, undecorated, lighted artificial tree with white star on top in the main entryway.
- *Stage-area:* Place a large advent wreath with appropriate white, pink, and blue candles and ribbons on the right side of the stage. On the left side, place a nine-foot tree decorated with a white star on top, white lights, silver stars, and pink and blue balls.
- *Image:* Do an image search for *newborn baby*. Choose a contemporary image that can have *We're Expecting* superimposed on it. If usable, fade image to use as background for lyrics to songs and Scripture. This image will be used for the large screen, the web page, and publicity posters for series.

PRIMING

- Two weeks before the series begins hang large pink or blue ribbons on sanctuary doors (the kind hung on the doors of new parents).
- Using bulletins, newsletters, e-mail, the church webpage, and announcements, begin to post the "We're Expecting" image described above.

- In conspicuous places around the church arrange baby items in groups of three (Examples- booties, diapers, and receiving blankets placed on a countertop). With each display, place a sign that reads something like this:
    - Booties $ 7.99
    - Receiving blankets $12.99
    - Diapers $15.98
    - New Life   Priceless
- One week before the series begins, request that everyone, including children, bring a baby picture of himself or herself on the first Sunday of Advent. Inform them that because the pictures will be used to decorate a tree in the entryway, they need to bring pictures that do not have to be returned. Photocopies are acceptable.

Week One: *EXPECT THE UNEXPECTED*
Matthew 1:18–21

Sermon in a sentence: Saying 'yes' to the new life God offers means being prepared for major life-changes.

Stations #1

SUPPLIES: Nine-foot lighted Christmas tree in the main entryway, white star for top, large table on which to work, glue sticks, pre-cut pieces of pink and blue cardstock (circles, squares, and rectangles, all about six inches across), hole punches, ink pens, and six-inch pieces of pink and blue ribbon.

INSTRUCTIONS: As people enter, invite them to help decorate the church for Christmas by mounting their baby picture on a piece of the pre-cut cardstock, tying a ribbon through it, and writing their name on the back before hanging it on the tree in the entryway. This 'family tree' will stay up through Advent.[1]

Station #2

SUPPLIES: Small table, note cards, ink pens, pushpins, a corkboard, large poster with the following text:

> *Mary and Joseph suddenly found themselves in an unexpected and unpopular place. Because they were unmarried and expecting a child, everyone assumed the worst about them. Gossip ran rampant. How do you think their faith community treated them during this time? What must life have been like for them in the midst of a scandal?*
>
> *Can you think of someone in your church or community who is living through a scandal right now? How have you treated them? Have you judged without knowing all the facts? Even if the gossip is true, is it your job to judge them? Have you passed on gossip? Have you made their lives even more uncomfortable by the way you have responded to them? Pray about this. Ask God what you can do to ease their burden. As you do, you may hear him say something very "Unexpected."*
>
> *Take a note card and write, "I'm sorry for the way I have judged you and treated you. Please forgive me. From this moment on, I commit to _____."*
> *Fold the card in half and pin it to the corkboard. As you carry out this commitment, thank God for allowing you to be an instrument that may help someone heal.*

---

[1] This personalized tree quickly became a center of interaction. People would stand around it looking at photos, trying to guess who they were, looking for their own and those of friends, admiring each other's children, and talking as they pointed photos out.

Station #3:

SUPPLIES: Table or kneelers, votives, candle lighter, large poster with the following text:

> *Mary and Joseph assumed that they would marry and live an ordinary, average life together. The events that unfolded were not what they were expecting. When they chose to follow God's leadership, they found themselves facing a time of confusion, fear, and distress.*
>
> *What about you? Is God asking you to go on an unexpected adventure? Is he trying to talk to you about changing your plans and trusting him to walk in faith to an unknown destination? Are you willing to let go of your own plans and instead walked down an unexpected path? Can you honestly say, as Mary did, "I am the Lord's servant . . . May it be to me as you have said," (Luke 1:38).*
>
> *Do you feel you need more light if you are to follow? If so, light a candle on the table. Pray, asking for God to help you trust Him enough to believe He is at work in your life even if you can't see it. Thank him for wanting to use you to show his love to the world.*

Station #4:

SUPPLIES: Table, pencils, copies of the matching game below (one per person), a large poster with the following text:

> *Those first few months of Mary's pregnancy, did Joseph ever doubt? Did he begin to wonder if God had ever really spoken to him? Did he question his own sanity at times? Did he have any lingering suspicions about Mary? Did he cling to the memory of the angelic visitation like a life preserver? Did he search the prophecies looking for*

verification? Imagine for a moment that you are in his shoes, hoping for something, anything, to substantiate what he wanted to believe was happening.

With this in mind, match each event on the left to a prophetic verse on the right that may have offered Joseph some peace of mind.

Matching Game

Caesar forces the couple to go to Bethlehem	**Hosea 11:1-** When Israel was a child, I loved him, and out of Egypt I called my son.
The visitation of the shepherds	**Isaiah 42:6-** I, the Lord, have called you in righteousness. I will take hold of your hand. I will keep you and make you to be a covenant for the people and a light for the nations.
The visitation of the Wise Men	**Micah 5:2-** But you, Bethlehem Ephrathah, though you are small among the clans of Judah, out of you will come for me one who will be ruler over Israel, whose origins are from of old, from ancient times."
The instructions to flee to Egypt	**Luke 2:8–17-** And there were shepherds living out in the fields nearby keeping watch over their flocks at night. An angel of the Lord appeared to them . . . and they were terrified. But the angel said to them, "Do not be afraid. I bring you good news that will cause great joy for all the people. Today in the town of David a Savior has been born to you; he is the Messiah, the Lord.

This will be a sign to you: You will find a baby wrapped in cl oths and lying in a manger." . . . So they hurried off and found Mary and Joseph, and the baby, who was lying in the manger. When they had seen him, they spread the word concerning what had been told them about this child.

Station #5:

SUPPLIES: Large sheet of butcher paper mounted on the wall, non-permanent markers, and large poster with the following text:

God doesn't seem to worry about going through the proper channels to get things done. When God spoke to Mary, he didn't say, "Now go work this out with Joseph and then we'll get started." Nor did he say, "You are just a minor so you need to ask your parent's permission first." He dealt directly with a young teenager who had no power in her culture or day, yet God gave her the power to accept or reject his desire for her life

What if God came to you and said, "This is what I want to do with your life, and when I do it, the world will change. Will you consent to come with me?"

What common excuses might people use to avoid saying 'yes'? Write one or two of those excuses on the butcher paper.

Pray, asking yourself, "Have I been using an excuse to say 'no' to God about something? What is it?" If God reveals something to you, ask, "Where do I go from here?"

Station #6

SUPPLIES: Small table, communion elements, large sign with the following text:

> *When God stepped through the barrier that separated the visible from the invisible, he stepped into the body of a woman. She gave birth to a real child with a physical body. He laughed, cried, ran, slept, ate, drank, caught colds, and skinned his knees.*
>
> *As an adult, he called himself The Bread of Life.*
>
> *Before he died, he took a loaf of bread and said, "This is my body, broken or you. This is my blood, poured out for you and for many for the forgiveness of sin. Every time you eat this bread or drink the cup, remember how much I love you."*
>
> *Take time to thank God for that selfless, unconditional love. Then receive his gift to you as you serve yourself communion*

ADDITIONAL ACTIVITIES USED DURING THE ADVENT SERIES

WEEK TWO: EXPECT DETOURS   Luke 2:1–7

Station

SUPPLIES: Six-foot-long strip of butcher paper mounted on wall, non-permanent markers, and large sign with the following text:

It is approximately sixty-nine miles from Nazareth to Bethlehem. Mary and Joseph had to walk that distance when she was a full nine-months pregnant.

Knowing that she would probably give birth during the trip, how do you think they packed for the journey? Remember that they couldn't check luggage, and there is no mention of Mary riding a donkey in the Gospel accounts of Jesus' birth. That idea came much later. Assuming they had to carry everything they needed in their hands or on their back, they had to pack lightly. What necessities do you think they packed?

Use your imagination for a moment and decide what five things you would have packed if you were in their position. Be realistic. Write your answer on the butcher paper.

Activity

Place a birth announcement/baby shower invitation in each seat in the sanctuary. (Cheap but attractive announcements can be found on sites such as *Snapfish* or *Shutterfly* for as little as forty cents each, or you can make your own).

On the front, print:

A STAR IS BORN!
*Introducing my beloved son, JESUS,
Conceived by My Holy Spirit,
Trusted to the care of Mary and Joseph
Born in the fullness of time.*

On the back, print:

As Christmas approaches, thousands of women find themselves facing unplanned pregnancies. While their stories are much different from that of Mary, they too need a place of understanding and a touch of grace.

You are invited to express God's grace to them by donating packages of newborn size disposable diapers. We will be collecting them over the course of December in the play-yard in the entryway. On New Year's Day, they will be shared with new mothers at _____*

* Fill in the blank with the name of the local indigent care hospital.

WEEK THREE: EXPECT NEW LIFE   Luke 2: 8–20

Station

SUPPLIES: Table on which to work, baby lotion, bag of cow manure from garden supply shop (broken open, placed beneath table, and lightly misted with water), hay strewn around floor, butcher paper taped to wall, non-permanent markers, large poster with the following text:

Today's hospitals do everything possible to remain sterile. Surfaces are scrubbed germ free. The smells are those of antiseptics. Stainless, glass, and plastic abound because they are easy to clean. After the birth, mother and child are comforted—a clean room, a warm bed with fresh sheets, special soaps and lotions. Smooth some baby lotion on your hands. Do you remember the unmistakable scent?

Mary did not have the advantages we do. She gave birth in the same room where animals were kept at night. Even in a more primitive time, that was NOT normal. Imagine her there—lying on the ground with no female family members to coach her through the birth.

Many women claim to experience heightened senses during labor. Sounds seem louder. The sense of touch is magnified. Smells are stronger. What do you suppose Mary was undergoing? Close your eyes and try to picture her labor and delivery room.

What do you think God was saying to humanity in choosing this setting to enter the world? Write your thoughts on the roll of butcher paper.

Station

SUPPLIES: Table, manger with hay, lined notebook paper, pens, and large sign with the following text:

Assume the role of Joseph for a moment. Old friends and family members were probably shunning him because of the 'illegitimate' pregnancy. If Joseph's parents were still living, they would have also returned to Bethlehem for the census, but there is no mention of grandparents at the manger.

Few men in those days had ever witnessed childbirth, yet Joseph found himself in the position of being Mary's midwife. What was he feeling? Had he asked some woman in advance what he should do during the delivery? Did he understand there were angels watching over the birth or did he panic at some point?

Take a sheet of paper and write a letter to God in Joseph's voice. What would you want to say to God if you were in his circumstances? When you have completed the letter, fold it and place it in the manger.

Station

SUPPLIES: Play-yard, poster with the following text:

> *Diapers for Newborns: After you place your donation in the play-yard, take a moment to pray for mothers who don't have the financial means to support their new child, for mothers whose children go to bed hungry, and for mothers who have no support system to help with child-rearing.*

WEEK FOUR: EXPECT OTHERS TO CELEBRATE WITH US

Mathew 2:1–11

Station

SUPPLIES: Table, note cards, pens, several dozen small gift boxes, birthday wrapping paper, curling ribbon, iPod softly playing *The Little Drummer Boy*, large poster with the following text:

> *Christmas gifts . . . How much time do you spend selecting them? How much do you spend on the person you love most?*

> *Have you ever considered giving a Christmas gift to Jesus? It is HIS birthday, not ours. What if you gave him something at least as expensive as the other gifts you give?*

> *Maybe you are in the position of the little drummer boy with very little to give financially. Even so, like him you have time and talents. Could you spend them working in a homeless shelter or prison ministry, visiting an elderly person with no family to speak of, or babysitting for a single mother so she can get away?*

Maybe you are in the position of the wise men with abundant material resources. How could you use them to show God's love to the least of these? Could you donate to a women's shelter, purchase Christmas gifts for a needy family, make a large donation to alleviate hunger locally or abroad, or pay college tuition for a needy student?

If you would like to commit to giving a gift to Jesus, take a notecard and write what your gift to him will be this year. Fold the notecard and place it in one of the boxes. Wrap it in the birthday paper. Add a bow. Place it under the tree in the entryway.

WEEK FIVE: EXPECT A CHANGE IN PRIORITIES

Matthew 2:1–12

Video to Introduce the Service

Video several younger fathers in the congregation answering the question, "How did your priorities change when your first child was born?" Edit to 4 minutes.

Station

SUPPLIES: Table, four-foot artificial tree, strips of colored paper (1"x8.5"), tape, markers, the beginning of a paper chain hung on tree, a large poster with the following text:

There are many things that can interrupt our lives—loss of a job, a family crisis, a broken relationship, a missed flight, a traffic jam, or a declined credit card. We usually respond to these interruptions with cries of frustration.

Mary and Joseph experienced a major interruption in their life when they were forced to flee their new home in the middle of the night to save their child's life. When God spoke, they left behind their newly established life in Bethlehem—their house, Joseph's growing carpentry business, and developing friendships. Because they did so, God led them to a place of safety.

Is anything threatening to interrupt your life right now? Write it on one of the strips of paper. How are you reacting to it? Are you angry, frustrated, or confused? Hold it in your hand as you continue to read.

Have you considered that sometimes not all the time the things that interrupt our lives are a type of Divine intervention? How can Mary and Joseph's flight to Egypt educate and inspire us today?

Take time to pray about your interruption, asking God if he is trying to say something to you through it. Much of the discontent we feel at life's interruptions comes from our disconnection from God. Listen to him. Is he telling you to flee a situation or to stay put? Does he want you to learn patience, to focus on today and not tomorrow, or perhaps to be more aware of his presence during the detour?

After praying, use the tape to add your strip of paper to the paper chain. What does the fact that it is part of a longer chain say to you?

Station

SUPPLIES: Laptops, copies of Thomas Merton's prayer (below), several cushions (to be used as kneelers), a large poster with the following text:

Sometimes burdens get piled on top of burdens. When Jesus was two years old, Mary and Joseph began a second major journey—this time to Egypt. It was NOT a short trip.

Using one of the laptops, pull up Mapquest. Look at the route from Bethlehem, Judea to Alexandria, Egypt. Much of the road leads through a brutal desert.

Are you walking an unfamiliar road, unsure of where you are going? Does it seem endless? Take one of the copies of Thomas Merton's prayer. Kneel on a cushion and silently or softly read the prayer. Read it repeatedly, letting the words sink in deep. Can you make it your own prayer?

Feel free to take a copy with you when you are through praying.

Thomas Merton's Prayer

My Lord God, I have no idea where I am going.

I do not see the road ahead of me.

I cannot know for certain where it will end.

Nor do I really know myself, and the fact that
    I think that I am following your will does
    not mean that I am actually doing so.

But I believe that the desire to please you
    does in fact please you. And I hope I have
    that desire in all that I am doing.

I hope that I will never do anything apart from that desire.
    And I know that if I do this you will lead me by the
    right road though I may know nothing about it.

Therefore will I trust you always though I may
seem to be lost and in the shadow of death.

I will not fear, for you are ever with me, and you
will never leave me to face my perils alone.

Amen

Appendix 2

ORDER OF WORSHIP: FIRST SUNDAY OF ADVENT

45 minutes before the service begins: Fir scented candles are lit in entryway and sanctuary.

30 minutes before the service begins: All Stations are open for use. Quiet music is playing in the background.

Prelude to Worship: Handbells, *Joy to the World*

>(As music plays, tree and candles in windows are lit by _____)

Call to Worship and Prayer: Jeremiah 31:31-34

>(Projected on screen while read from rear of sanctuary by _____ as one verse of *God Has Spoken by His Prophets* is softly played in the background)

Congregational Hymn: *God Has Spoken by His Prophets*

Lighting the Advent Candle of Hope:

>(Read by _____ on stage as a verse of *O Come, O Come Emmanuel* is softly played in background.)

The Christmas story summarizes all the expectations of the poor and insignificant people of the Old Testament who were waiting for the Messiah to come. They lived in the hope that God's promises would one day be fulfilled. When fulfillment finally came, it was first announced to them, to those poor and insignificant people, to Mary, to Joseph, and to the shepherds.

When the angels declared to them, "You have found God's favor," they all willingly entered into the story, into the universal dimension of God's saving grace. Mary expressed her hope in a beautiful song we call The Magnificat. Joseph expressed his hope in obedience, saying "Yes" to God and "Marry me anyway" to Mary. The shepherds expressed their hope in the words, "Let us go and see . . ." They all gave voice to hope. (Lights candle)

We live in a time that needs hope more than ever. It needs joyful, strong women and men who announce the Good News of God's Love. Let us join together now and voice our hope for God's Kingdom come—on earth as it is in heaven.

Congregational Hymn: *O Come, O Come Emmanuel*

Congregational Hymn: *Come, Thou Long Expected Jesus*

Prayers of the People: (Led by ––––––––– from rear of sanctuary)

Holy and gracious God,

We come to you admitting our fears for our own future and the future of those we love. When Mary and Joseph were in a similar place, you told them, "Do not be afraid." You tell us the same thing. Help us remember that we can be fearless because we have tasted the depth of your love for us. With confidence that you do care for us, we lift up before you these concerns:

> Individuals in congregation are given time to voice brief concerns aloud (Example: "The Stevens family," "The flood victims," "Our youth retreat") After each, the congregation responds, **"Lord, Hear our prayer."** After sufficient time is allowed, conclude with:

Father, these are real concerns. Free us from any lethargy that keeps us from doing anything about them. Stir us to devotion and action. Lead us out of preoccupation with our own problems and use us to reveal the love of Jesus Christ, in whose name we pray, to those around us. Amen.

Congregational Hymn: *While the World Awaited*

Sermon: *Expect the Unexpected*

Time of Response: (Quiet music plays during this time)

> Explain that if God is speaking to us, that he expects us to respond to his voice. The next ten minutes will be devoted to our individual responses. Assure them there is no right or wrong way to respond—that no two people will ever respond exactly the same way. Explain that they can remain in their seats to pray or mediate. They can also come to the front and pray at the altar, pray with one of several ministers stationed at the front, go to one or more of the stations and spend time there, place an offering in the basket at the back of the room, or serve themselves communion.

Congregational Hymn: *My Soul Rejoices*

Congregational Hymn: *Good News*

Benediction: (Led by _____ at the rear of sanctuary)

> *God has come. He is living among us. We have reason to rejoice. Remain watchful for him as you go about your Advent preparations. Live this week knowing he is with you, calling you to good works as you follow him. May the blessing of God——Father, Son and Holy Spirit——be with you now and forever. Amen.*

For thirty minutes following the service: Stations remain open while ministerial staff lingers in the sanctuary area to receive feedback and to fellowship with congregants.

Bibliography

Barna Group, "Barna Studies the Research, Offers a Year-in-Review Perspective." December 18, 2009. (accessed July 12, 2013).

Barnes, Rebecca, and Lindy Lowery. "Seven Startling Facts: An Up Close Look at Church Attendance in America." *Church Leaders* February 2013. http://www.churchleaders.com/pastors/pastor-articles/139575-7-startling-facts-an-up-close-look-at-church-attendance-in-america.html (accessed July 7, 2013).

Bassock, Miriam, Kevin N. Dunbar, and Keith J. Holyoak. "Introduction to the Special Section on the Neural Substrate of Analogical Reasoning and Metaphor Comprehension." *Journal of Experimental Psychology: Learning, Memory, and Cognition* 38, no. 2 (August, 2011): 261-263. http://0web.ebscohost.com.catalog.georgefox.edu/ ehost/ pdfviewer/ pdfviewer?sid=30cb94f9-403b-4a07-9ddf-6ed994bb8dbb%40sessionmgr 110&vid=6&hid-107 (accessed January 28, 2013).

Bergen, Benjamin K. *Louder Than Words: the New Science of How the Mind Makes Meaning*. New York, NY: Basic Books, 2012.

Brookfield, Stephen D. *Powerful Techniques for Teaching Adults*. San Francisco, CA: Jossey-Bass, 2013.

Bruce, Juliet. "This is Your Brain on Story." *Living Story Blogspot*, entry posted January 15, 2012, http://livingstory-ny.blogspot.

com/2012/01/this-is-your-brain-on-story.html (accessed September 13, 2012).

Caine, Renata Nummela, and Geoffrey Caine, "Understanding a Brain-Based Approach to Learning and Teaching," *Educational Leadership* 48, no. 2 (October 1990). http://www.ascd.org/ASCD/pdf/journals/ed lead/el199010caine.pdf (accessed October 18, 2011).

Cho, Eugene. "Death by Ministry." *Eugene Cho Blog* August 11, 2010. (accessed July 14, 2013).

Connell, J. Diane. "The Global Aspects of Brain-Based Learning," *Educational Horizons* 88, no. 1, Fall 2009.

Cron, Lisa. *Wired for Story: The Writer's Guide to Using Brain Science to Hook Readers from the Very First Sentence.* New York: Ten Speed Press, 2012.

Damasio, Antonio R. *Descartes' Error: Emotion, Reason, and the Human Brain.* London: Penguin, 2005.

DiSalvo, David. *What Makes Your Brain Happy and Why You Should Do the Opposite.* Amherst, NY: Prometheus Books, 2011.

Duarte, Nancy. *Resonate: Present Visual Stories That Transform Audiences.* Hoboken, NJ: Wiley, 2010.

Dyrness, William A. *Poetic Theology: God and the Poetics of Everyday Life.* Grand Rapids, MI: W.B. Eerdmans Pub. Co., 2011.

Fadel, Charles, and Chervl Lemke. "Multimodal Learning Through Media: What the Research Says." *Meteri Group, Commissioned by Cisco Systems* (2008) http://www.cisco.com/web/strategy/docs/education/Multimodal-Learning-Through-Media.pdf (accessed November 30, 2011).

Fanelli, Daniele. "How Many Scientists Fabricate and Falsify Research? A Systematic Review and Meta-Analysis of Survey Data," *PLOS ONE* September 24, 2009. http://www.plosone.org/article/info%3Adoi%2F10.1371%2Fjournal.pone.0005738 (accessed August 14, 2013).

Fromme, Eric. *Man for Himself: An Inquiry Into the Psychology of Ethics.* New York: Henry Holt & Co., 1947.

Geary, James. *I Is an Other: the Secret Life of Metaphor and How It Shapes the Way We See the World.* New York: Harper, 2011.

Gibbs Jr., Raymond W., ed. "Metaphor and Thought: The State of the Art." in *The Cambridge Handbook of Metaphor and Thought,* edited by Raymond W. Gibbs, Jr., 3-13. New York: Cambridge University Press, 2008.

Gottschall, Jonathan. *The Storytelling Animal: How Stories Make Us Human.* Boston: Houghton Mifflin Harcourt, 2012.

Grenny, Joseph. *Influencer: The New Science of Leading Change.* 2nd ed. Vitalsmarts. New York: McGraw-Hill Education, 2013.

Hartford Institute for Religion Research, *"Fast Facts about American Religion,"* (Hartford Seminary: Hartford, CT, 2012), http://hirr.hartsem.edu/research/fastfacts/fast_facts.html (accessed June 19, 2013).

Heschel, Abraham Joshua. *Noonday.* Vol. N526, *God in Search of Man: A Philosophy of Judaism.* New York: Farrar, Straus and Giroux, 1976, 1955.

Herz, Rachel S. "Odor-associative Learning and Emotion: Effects on Perception and Behavior," *Oxford Journals* 30, no. 1 (2005): 250-251.

Howes, David, ed., *Empire of the Senses: The Sensual Cultural Reader.* New York: Berg Publishers, 2005.

Jensen, Eric. *Brain-Based Learning: The New Paradigm of Teaching.* 2nd ed. Thousand Oaks, CA: Corwin Press, 2008.

Jordi, Richard. "Reframing the Concept of Reflection." *Adult Education Quarterly* 61, no 2 (2011): 7. http://aeq.sagepub.com/content/61/2/181. (Accessed April 10, 2011).

Kaufman, Geoff F., and Lisa K. Libby. "Changing Beliefs and Behavior Through Experience- Taking." *Journal of Personality and Social Psychology* 103, no. 1 (2012): 1-17. http://www.ncbi.nlm.nih.gov/pubmed/22448888 (accessed November 20, 2012).

Kress, Gunther R. *Multimodality: A Social Semiotic Approach to Contemporary Communication.* London: Routledge, 2010.

Laderman, Gary. "The Rise of Religious 'Nones' Indicates the End of Religion as We Know It." *The Huffington Post* March 20, 2013. http://www.huffingtonpost.com/gary-laderman/the-rise-of-religious-non b2913000.html (accessed April 2013).

Lakoff, George, and Mark Johnson. *Metaphors We Live By.* Chicago: University Of Chicago Press, 2003.

Lewis, Patrick J. "Storytelling as Research/Research as Storytelling." *Qualitative Inquiry* June 2011. http://qix.sagepub.com/content/17/6/505 (accessed November 24, 2012).

Lombardi, Judy. "Beyond Learning Styles: Brain-Based Research and English-Learners," *Clearing House: A Journal of Educational Strategies, Issues, and Ideas* 81, no. 5 (May/June 2008), 222.

Merrit, Carol Howard. "Tribal Church: Perspectives on the Young Clergy Crisis." *The Christian Century* December 10, 2011. http://

www.christiancentury.org/blogs/archive2011-2012/perspectives-young-clergy-crisis (accessed July 5, 2013).

Miller, Anne. *Metaphorically Selling: How to Use the Magic of Metaphors to Sell, Persuade, & Explain Anything to Anyone.* New York: Chiron Associates Inc, 2004.

McClung, Grant, "Pentecostals: The Sequel," *Christianity Today* (April 2006): 30.

Murray, Joddy. *Non-Discursive Rhetoric: Image and Affect in Multimodal Composition.* Albany: SUNY Press, 2009.

Pierson, Mark. *The Art of Curating Worship: Reshaping the Role of Worship Leader.* Minneapolis, MN: Sparkhouse Press, 2010.

Rognlien, Bob. *Experiential Worship: Encountering God with Heart, Soul, Mind, and Strength.* Colorado Springs, CO: NavPress, 2005.

Rosenblum, Lawrence D. *See What I'm Saying: The Extraordinary Powers of Our Five Senses.* New York, NY: W. W. Norton, 2010.

Ruell, Peter. "The Look of Music," *Harvard Gazette* August 19, 2013. (accessed August 21, 2013).

Rutledge, Pamela Brown. "The Psychological Power of Storytelling." *Psychology Today.* January, 2011. http://www.psychologytoday.com/blog/positively-media/201101/the-psychological-power-storytelling (accessed November 24, 2012).

Schlossberg, Edwin. *Interactive Excellence: Defining and Developing New Standards for the Twenty-First Century.* Library of Contemporary Thought. New York: Ballantine Pub., 1998.

Simons, Daniel, and Christopher Chabris, "Selective Attention Test," (Champaign, IL: ViscogProductions, 1999), http://www.youtube.com/watch?v=vJG698U2Mvo. (accessed May 25, 2013).

Smith, James K A. *Desiring the Kingdom: Worship, Worldview, and Cultural Formation* (*Cultural Liturgies*). Grand Rapids, MI: Baker Academic, 2009.

﹘﹘﹘ *Imagining the Kingdom: How Worship Works (Cultural Liturgies)*. Grand Rapids, MI: Baker Academic, 2013.

Stolovitch, Harold D., and Erica J. Keeps. *Telling Ain't Training.* 2nd ed. Alexandria, VA: ASTD Press, 2011.

﹘﹘﹘ *Beyond Telling Ain't Training Fieldbook: Methods, Activities, and Tools for Effective Workplace Learning.* Alexandria, VA: ASTD Press, 2005.

Sweet, Leonard I. *Eleven Genetic Gateways to Spiritual Awakening.* Nashville: Abingdon Press, 1998.

﹘﹘﹘ *Nudge: Awakening Each Other to the God Who's Already There.* Colorado Springs, CO: David C. Cook, 2010.

﹘﹘﹘ "Storytellers Change the World: A Film Review of 'Lincoln,'" *Beyond Evangelical: The Blog of Frank Viola*, entry posted December 7, 2012. http://frankviola.org/2012/12/07/ ; lincoln (accessed December 7, 2012).

﹘﹘﹘ *The Greatest Story Never Told: Revive Us Again.* Nashville, TN: Abingdon Press, 2012.

Sweet, Leonard I., and Frank Viola. *Jesus: A Theography.* Nashville, TN: Thomas Nelson, 2012.

Willard, Dallas. *The Divine Conspiracy: Rediscovering Our Hidden Life in God.* San Francisco: HarperSanFrancisco, 1998.

Williams, Jennifer. "Your Brain on Stories." *Verillance (n) Truth and Brilliance, Better Marketing Through Science*, entry posted February 28, 2011, (accessed November 3, 2012).

About the Author

Having begun her career as an educator, Paula Champion-Jones is well versed in educational theory. Having spent a lifetime in church, she know how poorly prepared the average minister is to teach and is aware of the dismal results of the teaching methods most often employed. As a United Methodist pastor, she has effectively employed brain-based learning methods in three churches. While working on a DMin degree at George Fox Seminary, she thoroughly researched the subject under the mentorship of Leonard Sweet.

Paula Champion-Jones began her career as an elementary teacher. While taking time off to raise children, she became involved in her church's education ministry, eventually pursuing a Master of Divinity in Biblical Studies through New Orleans Baptist Seminary. Upon graduation in 1993, she was the recipient of the American Bible Society Award for Scholarly Achievement in Biblical Studies.

In 2000, she responded to the call to pastor and returned to school for a second MDiv in Methodist Studies from Memphis Theological Seminary. Since 2002, she has served as a pastor in the United Methodist Church. During this time, she has focused on creative worship. In May of 2014 she completed her DMin at George Fox Seminary where she was presented with The Distinguished Dissertation Award. Her passion is making God more accessible to others during worship.

Paula lives with her husband of 42 years, Joseph Jones, in Hoover, Alabama. They have three adult daughters and three grandchildren. She is an avid reader, an amateur artist, and an enthusiastic flower gardener and storyteller.

CPSIA information can be obtained at www.ICGtesting.com
Printed in the USA
LVOW11s0033171014

409129LV00001B/103/P